For Grades 3–5

Literature
FOR EVERY
LEARNER

Differentiating Instruction With Menus for Poetry, Short Stories, and Novels

For Grades 3–5

Literature
FOR EVERY
LEARNER

Differentiating Instruction With Menus for Poetry, Short Stories, and Novels

Laurie E. Westphal

PRUFROCK PRESS INC.
WACO, TEXAS

Prufrock Press Inc.
P.O. Box 8813
Waco, TX 76714-8813
Phone: (800) 998-2208
Fax: (800) 240-0333
http://www.prufrock.com

TABLE OF CONTENTS

CHAPTER 1

Choice

C hanging
H ow
O verlooked
I ndividuals
C ommunicate
E xcellence

Choice in the Classroom

When considering choice in the classroom, we must first picture our classrooms and our curricula, including the wide range of abilities we may find within a single classroom. It has become increasing more popular to implement an inclusive, mixed-ability model. Teachers may find that their one classroom contains special needs students, on-level students, bilingual/ESL students, and gifted students, all wanting to be successful, all with different needs. Cipani (1995) stated it best in his assessment of the variety of needs found in these "inclusive" classrooms:

Students who are academically gifted, those who have had abundant experiences, and those who have demonstrated proficiency with lesson content typically tend to perform well when instruction is anchored at the "implicit" end of the instructional continuum. In contrast, low-performing students (i.e., students at risk for school failure, students with learning disabilities, and students with other special needs) and students with limited experience or proficiency with lesson content are most successful when instruction is explicit. Students with average academic performance tend to benefit most from the use of a variety of instructional methods that address individual needs. Instructional decisions for most students, therefore, should be based on assessment of individual needs. (p. 498–499)

Acknowledging that these varied and often contradictory needs arise within a mixed-ability setting can lead to frustration, especially when trying to design one assignment or task that can fit everyone's needs. There are few if any traditional, teacher-directed lessons that can be implicit, explicit, and based on individual needs all at the same time. There is, however, one *technique* that tries to accomplish this: the implementation of choice.

Choice: The Superman of Techniques?

Can the offering of appropriate choices really be the hero when our classrooms have such diversity of abilities? Can it leap buildings in a single bound and meet the needs of our implicit, explicit, and individual interests? If introduced properly, certainly it can. By considering the use and subsequent benefits of choice, it becomes apparent that by offering choices, teachers really can meet the needs of the range of students in such a diverse classroom setting. Ask adults whether they would prefer to choose what to do or be told what to do, and of course, they are going to say they would prefer to have a choice. Students have these same feelings. Although students may not always be experienced in making choices, just like adults, they will make choices based on their needs, which makes everyone involved in the classroom experience a little less stressed and frustrated.

> *"I wish I could build something for everything we do."*
>
> —Fourth-grade student, when asked what type of products she liked to create when given a choice

One benefit of choice is its ability to meet the needs of so many different students and their learning styles. Although choice is appropriate for all ability levels, it is especially well received by advanced and gifted students. The Dunedin College of Education (Keen, 2001) conducted a research study on the preferred learning styles and techniques of 250 gifted students. Students were asked to rank different learning options; of the 13 different options described to the students, only one option did not receive at least one negative response. It was the option of having choices. All students may have different learning styles and preferences, yet choice is the one option that meets all students' needs, as it moves past the idea that the teacher has the sole responsibility of deciding what is best for everyone. Students, whether they are gifted or have special needs, are going to choose what best fits their learning styles and educational needs.

> *"I got to make it like I wanted to make it. Mom wanted to help me but I told her I can do it myself!"*
>
> —Third-grade student, when asked how he felt about a diorama he had created

Another benefit of choice is a greater sense of independence for the students, as some of them have not had the opportunity to consider their own learning in the past. What a powerful feeling! Students will have the opportunity to design and create products based on their own vision, rather than what their teacher envisions for them. When using choice, there is a possibility for more than one "right" product; everyone can make the task he or she has selected his or her own, no matter his or her level of ability. When students would enter my classroom, they often had been trained by previous teachers to produce exactly what the teacher wanted, not what the students thought would be best. Teaching my students that what they envision could be correct (and incredible) was often a struggle. "Is this what you want?" or "Is this right?" were popular questions as we started the school year. After being offered various choice opportunities and experiencing the success that often accompanies their producing quality products that they envision, the students begin to take the responsibility for their work. Allowing students to have choices in the products they create to show their learning helps create independence at any age, or within any ability level.

> *"Can I use these [holding up questions written during an activity] when I make my poster?"*
>
> —Fifth-grade student

Strengthened student focus on the required content is a third benefit. When students have choice in the activities or products they wish to complete, they tend to be more focused on the learning process, which leads to the creation of their choice. Students become excited when they learn information that can help them develop a product they would like to create. This excitement can manifest in thought-provoking questions and discussions during a class rather than just hurrying through instruction so they can get to the homework. Students will pay closer attention to instruction when they have an immediate application for the knowledge being presented in class. It is also important to note that if students are focused, they are less likely to be off task during instruction as well.

The final benefit (and I am sure there are many more) is the simple fact that by offering varied choices at appropriate levels, implicit instructional options (and their counterpart, explicit instructional options), as well as individual needs, can be addressed without anyone getting overly frustrated or overworked. Many a great educator has referred to the idea that the best learning takes place when the students have a desire to learn and can feel successful during the process. Some students have a desire to be taught information, others prefer to explore and learn things that are new to them; still others do not want to learn anything unless it is of interest to them. By incorporating different activities from which to choose, students can stretch beyond what they already know, and teachers can create a void that needs to be filled in order for students to complete a product they have selected for themselves. This void leads to a desire to learn.

A Point to Ponder: Making Good Choices Is a Skill

"That [good choices as a skill] makes a lot of sense. I think I assume they should know how to make choices by now but they don't. Maybe they just aren't 'skilled' enough yet."

—Fourth-grade teacher, using air quotes to discuss choice as a skill

When we consider making good choices as a skill, much like writing an effective paragraph, it becomes easy enough to understand the processes needed to encourage students to make their own choices. In keeping with this analogy, students could certainly figure out how to write on their own, perhaps even how to compose sentences and paragraphs by modeling other examples. Imagine, however, the progress and strength of the writing produced when students are given guidance and even the most basic of instruction on how to accomplish the task. Even with instruction from the teacher, the written piece is still their own, but the quality of the finished piece is so much stronger when guidance is provided during the process. The same is true with the quality of choices students can make when it comes to their instruction and showing their level of knowledge in the classroom.

As with writing, students could make their own choices; however, when the teacher provides background knowledge and assistance, the choices become more meaningful and the products a student chooses to create become richer. Certainly all students need guidance in the choice-making process, but sometimes our on-level and special needs students may need the most help; they may not have been in an educational setting that has allowed them to experience different products and the idea of choice can be new to them. Some students may only have experienced basic instructional choices like choosing between two journal prompts or perhaps the option of making a poster or a PowerPoint about the content being studied. Other students may not have experienced even this level of choice. This can cause frustration for both teacher and student.

Teaching Choices as a Skill

So what is the best way to provide this guidance and develop the skill of making good choices? First, select the appropriate number of choices for your students. Although the goal may be to have students choose between nine different options, teachers might start by having their students choose between three predetermined choices the first day (if they were using a shape menu, students might choose a circle activity). Then, after those products have been created and submitted to grading, students can choose between another three options a few days later, and another three perhaps the following week. By breaking the choices into smaller manageable pieces, teachers are reinforcing how to approach a more complex and/or varied situation that involves choice in the future. All students can work up to making complex choices with longer lists of options as their choice skill-level increases.

Second, students will need guidance on how to select the option that is best for them. They may not automatically gravitate toward varied options without an excited and detailed description of each choice. For the most part, students have been trained to produce what the teacher requests, which means that when given a choice, they will usually choose what they think will please the teacher. That means that when the teacher discusses the different menu options, the teacher will need to be as equally excited about each. The discussion of the different choices has to be animated and specific. For example, if the content is all very similar, the focus would be on the product: "If you want to do some singing, this one is for you!" or "If you want to write and draw, mark this one as a maybe!" Sometimes, choices may differ based on both content and product, in which case, both can be pointed out to students to assist them in making a good choice. "You have some different choices for this story's menu, if you would like work with creating new endings as well as drawing, check this one as a maybe. If you are thinking you want to act and work with the characters, this one might be for you!" This thinking aloud or teacher feedback helps the students begin to see how they might approach different choices. The more exposure they have to the processing the teacher provides, the more skillful they become in their choice making.

How Can Teachers Provide Choices?

"I have seen my behavior issues significantly decrease when my students have choices. I wasn't expecting that at all—I thought they would be off task."

—Fifth-grade inclusion teacher, when asked how his special needs students respond to having choices

When people go to a restaurant, the common goal is to find something on the menu to satisfy their hunger. Students come into our classrooms having a hunger as well—a hunger for learning. Choice menus are a way of allowing our students to choose how they would like to satisfy that intellectual hunger. At the very least, a menu is a list of choices that students use to select an activity (or activities) they would like to complete in order to show what they have learned. At best, it is a complex system in which a student earns points toward a goal determined by the teacher or the student. The points are assigned to products based on the different levels of Bloom's revised taxonomy and the choices may come from different areas of study. If possible, a menu should also incorporate a free-choice option for those "picky eaters" who would like to make a special order to satisfy their needs.

The next few sections provide examples of different menu formats that will be used in this book. Each menu has its own benefits, limitations or drawbacks, and time considerations. An explanation of the free-choice option and its management will follow the information on each type of menu.

Three Shape Menu

> *"I like the flexibility of the three shape menu. I can give students just one strip of shapes or the entire menu depending on their readiness."*
>
> —Third-grade teacher

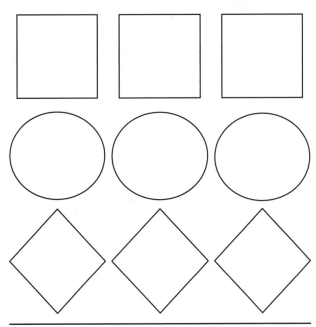

Figure 1.1. Three Shape menu.

Description

The Three Shape menu (see Figure 1.1) is a basic menu with a total of nine predetermined choices for students. The choices are created at the various levels of Bloom's revised taxonomy (Anderson & Krathwohl, 2001) and incorporate different learning styles. All products of the same shape carry the same weight for grading and have similar expectations for completion time and effort.

Benefits

Flexibility. This menu can cover one topic in depth, or three different aspects of a topic. When this menu covers just one objective, students have the option of completing three products: one from each shape "group."

Friendly design. Students quickly understand how to use this menu. It is easy to explain how to make the choices based on the various shapes and the shapes can be used to visually separate expectations (i.e., circles the first day, squares the next.)

Weighting. All products are equally weighted, so recording grades and maintaining paperwork is easily accomplished with this menu.

Short time period. This menu is intended for shorter periods of time, between 1–3 weeks.

Limitations

Few topics. This menu only covers one or three topics.

Time Considerations

This menu usually is intended for shorter amounts of completion time—at the most, they should take 3 weeks. If it focuses on one topic in-depth, the menu could be completed in one week.

Poetry Shape Menu

Description

The Poetry Shape menu (see Figure 1.2) is a menu that has been specifically designed for poems. Its format is unique, as it allows teachers to determine whether to provide three, six, or nine choices for their students. The number of choices is often determined by the amount of time the teacher plans to spend with the study of the work. The choices are created at the various levels of Bloom's revised taxonomy (Anderson & Krathwohl, 2001) and incorporate different learning styles. All products within the same row carry the same weight for grading and have similar expectations for completion time and effort.

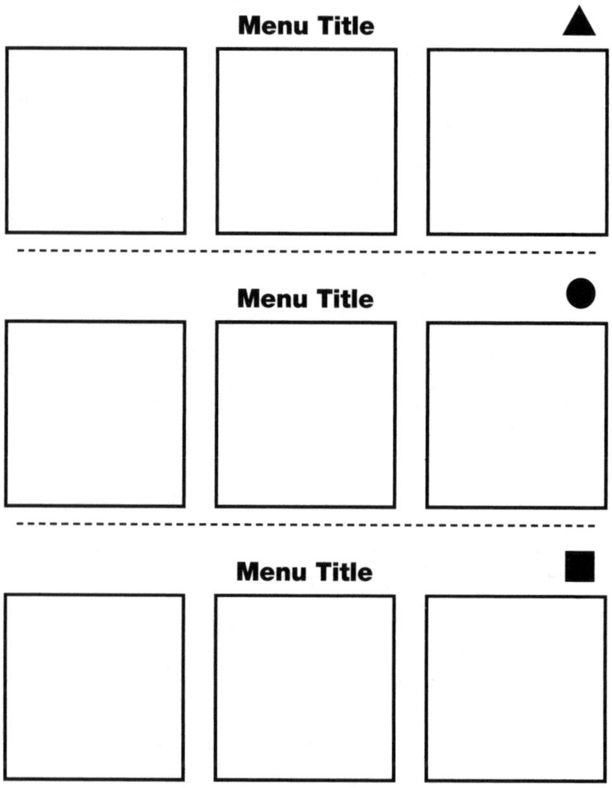

Benefits

Flexibility. This menu offers the opportunity for students to create one, two, or three products based on the amount of time spent on the study of the poem. If the teacher only has time for students to create one product, he may give students a strip of choices (▲, ●, ■) that have been tiered based on modifications

Friendly design. Students quickly understand how to use this menu. It is easy to explain how to make the choices based on the divisions located on the page.

Weighting. All products are equally weighted, so recording grades and maintaining paperwork are easily accomplished with this menu.

Menu Title ▲

Menu Title ●

Menu Title ■

Figure 1.2. Poetry Shape menu.

Short time period. This menu is intended for a short period of time, at most one week.

Limitations

None.

Time Considerations

This menu usually is intended for a short amount of completion time, based on the amount of time spent on the poem—at the most, they should take one week. If the teacher chooses to provide students with a single tiered ability strip, it could be completed in one or two class periods.

Tic-Tac-Toe Menu

"Sometimes I only liked two, but I had to do three."

—Second-grade student, when asked what he liked least about a menu used in his classroom

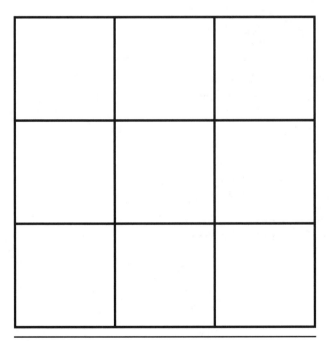

Figure 1.3. Tic-Tac-Toe menu.

Description

The Tic-Tac-Toe menu (see Figure 1.3) is a well-known, commonly used menu that contains a total of eight predetermined choices and, if appropriate, one free choice for students. Choices can be created at the same level of Bloom's revised taxonomy (Anderson & Krathwohl, 2001), or be arranged in such a way as to allow for the three different levels or even three different content areas. If all of the choices have been created at the same level of Bloom's revised taxonomy, each choice carries the same weight for grading and has similar expectations for completion time and effort.

Benefits

Flexibility. This menu can cover one topic in depth, or three different topics, objectives, or even content areas. When this menu covers just one objective and all tasks are from the same level of Bloom's revised taxonomy, students have the option of completing three projects in a tic-tac-toe pattern, or simply picking three from the menu. When it covers three objectives or different levels of Bloom's revised taxonomy, students will need to complete a tic-tac-toe pattern (either a vertical column or horizontal row) to be sure they have completed one activity from each objective or level.

Stretching. When students make choices on this menu that complete a row or column, based on its design, they will usually face one choice that is out of their comfort zone, be it through its level of Bloom's revised taxonomy, product learning style, or content. They will complete this "uncomfortable" choice because they want to do the other two options in that row or column.

Friendly design. Students quickly understand how to use this menu. It is nonthreatening because it does not contain points, and therefore seems to encourage students to stretch from their comfort zone.

Weighting. All projects are equally weighted, so recording grades and maintaining paperwork are easily accomplished with this menu.

Short time period. This menu is intended for shorter periods of time, between 1–3 weeks.

Limitations

Few topics. This menu only covers one or three topics.

Student compromise. Although this menu does allow for choice, a student will sometimes have to compromise and complete an activity he or she would not have chosen because it completes the required tic-tac-toe. (This is not always bad, though!)

Time Considerations

This menu usually is intended for shorter amounts of completion time—at the most, this menu should take 3 weeks with one product submitted each week. If a tic-tac-toe menu focuses on one topic in-depth and the students have time in class to work on their products, the menu could be completed in one week.

Meal Menu

> *"I really wanted to get to the dessert so I could make a board game. I had to do alot [sic] of stuff before I could make it. I like this menu."*
>
> —Third-grade student, when asked about what she liked, or did not like about the newest menu

Description

The Meal menu (see Figure 1.4) is a menu with a total of at least nine predetermined choices as well as two or more enrichment/optional activities for students. The choices are created at the various levels of Bloom's revised taxonomy (Anderson & Krathwohl, 2001) and incorporate different learning styles, with the levels getting progressively higher and more complex as students progress from breakfast to lunch and then to dinner. All products carry the same weight for grading and have similar expectations for completion time and effort. The enrichment or optional dessert options can be used for extra credit or replace another meal option at the teacher's discretion.

Breakfast
- ❑ ______________________
- ❑ ______________________
- ❑ ______________________

Lunch
- ❑ ______________________
- ❑ ______________________
- ❑ ______________________

Dinner
- ❑ ______________________
- ❑ ______________________
- ❑ ______________________

Dessert
- ❑ ______________________
- ❑ ______________________

Figure 1.4. Meal menu.

Benefits

Great starter menu. This menu is very straightforward and easy to understand, so time is saved in presenting the completion expectations.

Flexibility. This menu can cover either one topic in depth or three different objectives or aspects within a topic, with each meal representing a different aspect. With this menu, students have the option of completing three products: one from each meal.

Optional enrichment. Although not required, the dessert category of the meal menu allows students to have the option of going further or deeper if time during the unit permits.

Chunkability. The meal menu is very easy to break apart into smaller pieces. Whether you have students who need support in making choices or you only want to focus on one aspect of a story at a time, this menu can accommodate these decisions. Students could be asked to select a breakfast while the rest of the menu is put on hold until the breakfast product is submitted, then a lunch product is selected, and so on.

Friendly design. Students quickly understand how to use this menu because of its real-world application.

Weighting. All products are equally weighted, so recording grades and maintaining paperwork are easily accomplished with this menu.

Short time period. This menu is intended for shorter periods of time, between 1–3 weeks.

Limitations

None.

Time Considerations

The Meal menu usually is intended for shorter amounts of completion time—at the most, they should take 3 weeks with students working outside of class and submitting one product each week. If a menu focuses on one topic in-depth and the students have time in class to work on their products, the menu could be completed in one week.

List Menu

"At first I thought I had to do them all, and it was too much! Then [teacher] said we could pick what we wanted to get 100. I liked being able to pick from so many things."

—Fifth-grade student, when asked how he felt about a recent List menu

Description

The List menu (see Figure 1.5), or Challenge List, has a total of at least 10 predetermined choices, each with its own point value, and at least one free choice for students. Choices are simply listed with assigned points based on the levels of Bloom's revised taxonomy (Anderson & Krathwohl, 2001). The choices carry different weights and have different expectations for completion time and effort. A point criterion is set forth that equals 100%, and students choose how they wish to attain that point goal. There are two versions of the List menu included in this book: the Challenge List (one topic in depth) and the Three-Topic List menu (which, based on its structure, can accommodate multiple topics).

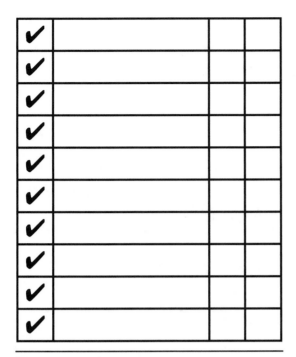

Figure 1.5. List menu.

Benefits

Responsibility. Students have complete control over their grades. They really like the idea that they can guarantee their grades if they complete their required work and meet the expectations set forth in the rubric. If students do not earn full credit on one of the chosen products, they can complete another to be sure they have met their goal. This responsibility over their own grades also allows a shift in thinking about grades—whereas students may think of grades in terms of how the teacher judged their work, or what the teacher gave them, having control over their grades leads students to understand that they earn their grades.

Different learning levels. This menu also has the flexibility to allow for individualized contracts for different learning levels within the classroom. Because there can be many ability levels within a classroom, it may be necessary to contract students based on their ability or even results from the pretesting of content. In which case, each student can contract for a certain number of points for his or her 100%.

Concept reinforcement. This menu also allows for an in-depth study of material; however, with the different levels of Bloom's revised taxonomy being represented, students who are still learning the concepts can choose some of the lower level point value products to reinforce the basics before jumping into the higher-level activities.

Variety. A List menu offers a larger variety of product choices. There is guaranteed to be a product of interest to everyone. (And if there isn't, there is always free choice!)

Limitations

One topic. This menu is best used for one topic in depth, so that students don't miss any specific content.

Preparation. Teachers need to have all materials ready at the beginning of the unit for students to be able to choose any of the activities on the list, which requires advanced planning.

Time Considerations

The List menu usually is intended for shorter amounts of completion time—at the most, 2 weeks. (*Note*: Once the materials are assembled, the preparation is minimal!)

2-5-8 Menu

> *"My favorite menu is the 2-5-8 kind. It's easy to understand and I can pick just what I want to do."*
>
> —Fourth-grade student, when asked about his favorite type of menu

Description

A 2-5-8 menu (see Figure 1.6) is a variation of a List menu, with a total of at least eight predetermined choices: two choices with a point value of 2, at least four choices with a point value of 5, and at least two choices with a point value of 8. Choices are assigned points based on the levels of Bloom's revised taxonomy (Anderson & Krathwohl, 2001). Choices with a point value of 2 represent the remember and understand levels, choices with a point value of 5 represent the apply and analyze levels, and choices with a point value of 8 represent the evaluate and create levels. All levels of choices carry different weights and have different expectations for completion time and effort. Students are expected to earn 10 points for a 100%. Students choose what combination they would like to use to attain that point goal.

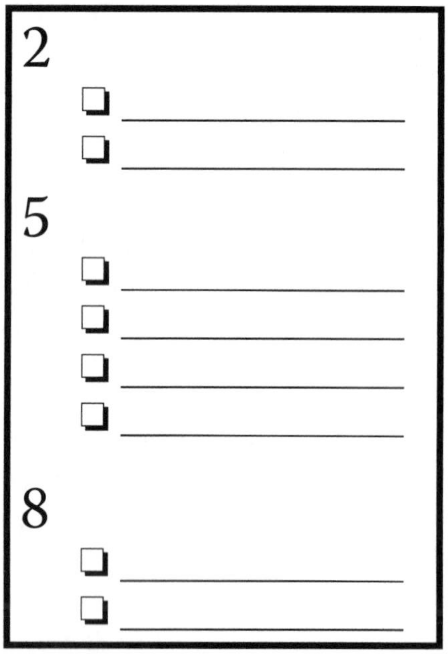

Figure 1.6. 2-5-8 menu.

Benefits

Responsibility. With this menu, students have complete control over their grades.

Low stress. This menu is one of the shortest menus and if students choose well, only requires students to complete two products. This menu is usually not as daunting as some of the longer, more complex menus. It provides students a great introduction into the process of making choices.

Guaranteed activity. This menu's design is also set up in such a way that students must complete at least one activity at a higher level of Bloom's revised taxonomy in order to reach their point goal.

Limitations

One topic. This menu works best with in-depth study of one topic.

Higher level thinking. Students usually choose to complete only one activity at a higher level of thinking.

Time Considerations

The 2-5-8 menu usually is intended for a shorter amount of completion time—at the most, one week.

Game Show Menu

> *"This menu really allowed me to compact for my students since I have so many different levels in my classroom. As students showed me they understood new concepts, they were allowed to work on their class work and then the column of the Game Show menu available for that day. It was such a motivator!"*
>
> —Fourth-grade science/math teacher

Description

The Game Show menu (see Figure 1.7) is a complex menu. It covers multiple topics or objectives with at least four predetermined choices and a free student choice for each objective. Choices are assigned points based on the levels of Bloom's revised taxonomy (Anderson & Krathwohl, 2001). All choices carry different weights and have different expectations for completion time and effort. A point criterion is set forth that equals 100%. Students must complete at least one activity from each objective in order to reach their goal.

Benefits

Free choice. This menu allows the most free choice options of any of the menu formats. Although it has many choices for students, if they do not want to complete the offered activities, they can propose their own activity for each objective on the menu.

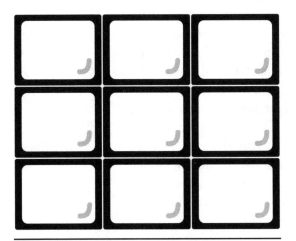

Figure 1.7. Game Show menu.

Responsibility. This menu allows students to guarantee their own grades.

Different learning levels. It has the flexibility to allow for individualized contracts for different learning levels within the classroom. Each student can contract for a certain number of points for his or her 100%.

Objectives guaranteed. The teacher is guaranteed that the students complete an activity from each objective covered, even if it is at a lower level.

Limitations

Confirm expectations. The only real limitation here is that students (and parents) must understand the guidelines for completing the menu.

Time Considerations

This menu usually is intended for a longer amount of completion time. Although they can be used as a yearlong menu (each column could be a grading period), they are usually intended for 2–3 weeks.

Free Choice in the Mixed-Ability Classroom

"Free choice? What do you mean? I don't get it."

—Fourth-grade special needs student

Most of the menus included in this book allow students to submit a free choice as a product. This free choice is a product of their choosing that addresses the content being studied and shows what the student has learned about the topic. Although this option is offered, students may not fully understand its benefits or immediately respond to the opportunity even after it has been explained. Although certain students may have experienced choice before and may be very excited by the idea of taking charge of their own learning, other students, especially those with special needs, may not have had much exposure to this concept. Their educational experiences tend to be objective based and teacher driven. This is not to say that these students would not respond well to the idea of free choice, in fact, they can embrace it as enthusiastically as gifted students. The most significant difference between these two groups successfully approaching free choice; is the amount of content needed by the student before she embarks on her proposed option. Special needs students need to feel confident in their knowledge of the content and information before they are ready to step out on their own, propose their own idea, and create their unique product.

The menus in this book that include a free choice option require that students submit a free choice proposal form for their teacher's consideration. Figure 1.8 shows two sample proposal forms that have been used many times successfully in my mixed-ability classroom. The form used is based on the type of menu being presented. If students are using the Tic-Tac-Toe, Meal, or Three Shape menu, there is no need to submit a point proposal form. A copy of these forms should be provided to each student when a menu is first introduced. A discussion should be held with the students so they understand the expectations of a free choice. If students do not want to make a proposal using the proposal form after the teacher has discussed the entire menu and its activities, they can place the unused form in a designated place in the classroom. Other students may want to use the form, and it is often surprising who wants to submit a proposal form after hearing about the opportunity!

Proposal forms must be submitted before students begin working on their free-choice products. The teacher then knows what the student should be working on and the student knows the expectations the teacher has for that product. Once approved, the forms can easily be stapled to the student's menu sheet for reference during the creation and grading process. The student can refer to it as he or she develops his or her free-choice product, and when the grading takes place, the teacher can refer to the proposed agreement for the "graded" features of the product.

Each part of the proposal form is important and needs to be discussed with students:

- *Name/Teacher's Approval.* The student must submit this form to the teacher for approval. The teacher will carefully review all of the information, discuss any suggestions or alterations with the student, if needed, and then sign the top.
- *Points Requested.* Found only on the point-based menu proposal form, this is where negotiation may need to take place. Students usually will submit their first request for a very high number (even the 100% goal). They tend to equate the amount of time a product will take with the amount of points it should earn. Please note, however, that the points are always based on the levels of Bloom's revised taxonomy. For example, a PowerPoint presentation with a vocabulary word quiz would get minimal points, although it may have taken a long time to create. If the students have not been exposed to the levels of Bloom's revised taxonomy, this can be difficult to explain. You can always refer to the popular "Bloom's Verbs" to help explain the difference between time requirements and higher level activities.

Name: _____   Teacher's Approval: _____

Free-Choice Proposal Form for Point-Based Menu

Points Requested: _____   Points Approved: _____

Proposal Outline

1. What specific topic or idea will you learn about?

2. What criteria should be used to grade it? (Neatness, content, creativity, artistic value, etc.)

3. What will your product look like?

4. What materials will you need from the teacher to create this product?

Name: _____   Teacher's Approval: _____

Free-Choice Proposal Form

Proposal Outline

1. What specific topic or idea will you learn about?

2. What criteria should be used to grade it? (Neatness, content, creativity, artistic value, etc.)

3. What will your product look like?

4. What materials will you need from the teacher to create this product?

Figure 1.8. Sample proposal forms for free choice.

- *Points Approved.* Found only on the point-based menu proposal form, this is the final decision recorded by the teacher once the point haggling is finished.
- *Proposal Outline.* This is where the student will tell you everything about the product he or she intends to complete. These questions should be completed in such a way that you can really picture what the student is planning on creating. This also shows you that the student has thought out what he or she wants to create.
  - o *What specific topic or idea will you learn about?* Students need to be specific here. It is not acceptable to just write "reading" or the title of the novel, story, or poem. This is where they look at the objectives or standards of the unit and choose which one their product demonstrates.
  - o *What criteria should be used to grade it?* Although there are guidelines for most of the products that the students might create, it is important for the students to explain what criteria are most important to evaluate the product. The student may indicate that the guidelines being used for the predetermined project is fine; however, he or she may also want to add other criteria here.
  - o *What will your product look like?* It is important that this be as detailed as possible. If a student cannot express what it will "look like," then he or she has probably not given the free-choice plan enough thought.
  - o *What materials will you need from the teacher to create this product?* This is an important consideration. Sometimes students do not have the means to purchase items for their project. This can be negotiated, as well, but if you ask what students may need, then they often will develop even grander ideas for their free choice.

CHAPTER 2

How to Use Menus in the Classroom

There are different ways to use instructional menus in the classroom. In order to decide how to implement a menu, the following questions should be considered:

- How much prior knowledge of the topic being taught do the students have before the unit or lesson begins?
- How confident are your students in making choices and working independently?
- How much intellectually appropriate information is readily available for students to obtain on their own?

After considering these questions, it becomes easier to determine how menus can be best implemented.

Building Background Knowledge or Accessing Prior Knowledge

"I have students with so many different experiences—sometimes I spend more time than I allotted to review and get everyone up to speed before we get started."

—Social studies teacher

There are many ways to use menus in the classroom. One way that is often overlooked is using menus to access or build background knowledge before a unit begins. This is frequently used when students have had exposure to upcoming content in the past, perhaps during the previous year's instruction, or through similar life experiences. Although they may have been exposed to the content previously, students may not remember the content details at the level needed to proceed with this year's instruction immediately. A shorter menu (the 2-5-8 menu is great for this) covering the previous years' objectives can be provided during the week prior to the new unit so students have the opportunity to recall and engage the information in a meaningful way before they are put on the spot to use it. Students are then ready to take it to a deeper level during this year's unit. For example, a week before starting a unit on *Mr. Popper's Penguins*, the teacher may use a short menu on penguins, knowing that the students may have had the content in the past and should be able to successfully work independently on the menu by engaging their prior knowledge. By offering a menu on the characteristics of penguins, students will have a greater understanding of the animals in the novel, and very little class time was taken for the prenovel background work. Students can work on products from the menu as anchor activities and homework throughout the week prior to the *Mr. Popper's Penguins* unit, with all products being submitted prior to its initiation. The students have been in the "penguin frame of mind" independently for at least one week and are ready to begin the novel.

Enrichment and Supplemental Activities

"I have some students who are always finishing early. I hate to just have them read ahead or do more questions since they end up finishing the novel before everyone else, which can cause its own set of frustrations."

—Reading teacher

Integrating menus into instruction for enrichment and as supplementary activities are the most common uses for menus in the classroom. In this case, the students usually do not have a lot of background knowledge and the intellectually appropriate information about the topic may not be readily available to all students. The teacher will introduce the menu and the activities at the beginning of a unit. The teacher will then progress through the necessary content at the normal rate, using his or her own curricular materials and periodically allowing class time and homework time throughout the unit for students to work on their menu choices to supplement a deeper understanding of the information being presented. This method is very effective, as it builds in an immediate use for the information the teacher is covering. For example, at the beginning of a novel unit on *Charlotte's Web*, the teacher many introduce the menu with the explanation that students may have not read enough of the novel to complete all of their choices yet. During the unit, however, as they read further, they will be prepared to work on the choices in which they are interested. If students want to work ahead, they certainly can read ahead of the class, but that is not required. Although gifted students often see this as a challenge and will begin to tear through a novel before the teacher discusses each chapter, special needs students begin to develop questions about upcoming events and are ready to ask them when the class gets to that point in the novel. As teachers, we often fight the battle of having students read ahead or "come to class prepared to discuss and question." By introducing a menu at the beginning of a novel and allowing students to complete products as reading progresses, the students naturally begin looking forward and come to class prepared without it being a completely separate requirement.

Mainstream Instructional Activities

> *"I really liked the flexibility of my menu. I rarely have the chance to work with small groups anymore and I miss it. I used a mix of whole group, small group and independent work."*
>
> —Fifth-grade reading/social studies teacher

Another option for using menus and choice in the classroom is to replace some whole-class curricular activities the teacher uses to teach certain aspects of a novel. In this case, the students may have some limited background knowledge about literary elements and information is readily available for them in their classroom resources. The teacher would pick and choose which aspects must be directly taught to the students in the large group or in small groups and which could be appropriately learned and reinforced through product menus. The novel unit is then designed using formal instructional large-group lessons, smaller informal group lessons, and specific menu days where the students will use the menu independently to reinforce the prior knowledge they already have learned. In order for this option to be effective, the teacher must feel very comfortable with the students' prior knowledge level, their reading levels, and their readiness to work independently.

Flipped Classroom Activities

> *"I wanted to try flipped instruction but was not too sure about the classroom aspect. A colleague recommended using a menu for my time with the students . . . it made such a difference."*
>
> —Fourth-grade self-contained teacher

The idea of choice fits hand-in-hand with the philosophy of flipped instruction or the flipped classroom model. When using flipped instruction, the goal is that the students acquire basic information needed through outside sources such as videos, PowerPoints, or other sources their teacher has selected for them. In the case of a novel study, rather than reading the novel aloud round-robin format, students will be responsible for reading sections of the book independently, outside of the classroom. This may mean the students are simply sitting down at home and reading to themselves, they may be watching a video of the story being read by the author, or listening to an audio recording of the necessary pages. No matter how they have "read" the pages, when the students return to class, their time is spent on quality activities and products based on their reading outside of the classroom. Because the methods students use to read the material are varied, logically, it would work best if the activities within the classroom are varied as well. Using a menu of options to offer and manage the activities and processing experiences will allow all of the different ability levels within the classroom to feel successful.

Using Leveled Menus With Your Students

"How am I going to handle it when students notice that the menu they have is different than one their classmate has?"

—Fifth-grade teacher

This book contains tiered or leveled menus for each of the included novels, stories, or poems. Although the reading material is the same, each of the three menus may have different values assigned to the same task, slightly different wording for similar tasks, the same product options in a different format, or even tasks that are only available on certain menus. All of these small modifications make certain menus more appropriate for different students based on their readiness, interest, and ability levels.

As we all know, students tend to compare answers, work, and ideas, and their choices on menus are not any different. Although students may notice the slight differences mentioned above, it may not be an issue when students are working in ability groups, as students are comfortable with having different options based on their grouping. It may also not be an issue when the menus are presented matter-of-factly, stating that everyone is getting a menu that was specifically selected for him or her. Students should rest assured that target numbers (goal of 100 is a 100%) are equal for all of the menus provided and the activities often perceived as the "best" or "most fun" by students are found on all of the version of the menu. Students should also know that most of the menus have a free choice proposal option so if they really want to do one of the activities found on another menu in the classroom, they are welcome to submit that activity on a free choice proposal form. By presenting tiered menus with confidence and an air for uniquely selecting each menu for its recipient, students are usually willing to proceed with the menu they have received.

> ### *"That's not fair . . ."*
>
> —Said by at least one student every second
> in classrooms across the nation

That being said, you may still have a few students who say (in a somewhat nasal and accusatory tone), "That's not fair!" When I first starting using leveled menus, I heard a few comments like this. They quickly dissipated with my standard and practiced responses. Of course the first response (which they do not always appreciate) is that fair is not equal. I know students do not like to hear this response as it is hard to argue against this, because it is patently true. Secondly, I remind students that everyone has different strengths and the menus are distributed based on everyone's strengths. Again, they know this; they just do not like to acknowledge it. Lastly, if the students are being especially surly, I sometimes have to play the "parent card," meaning, I am the teacher and I have the right to do what I feel is best for each student. This last option is nonnegotiable and although students may not like it, they understand the tone and sentiment as they have usually experienced it before at home.

The bottom line when it comes to using tiered menus is that students will respond to the use of seemingly different menus within one classroom based on how the teacher presents or reacts to it. In the past, when I have used different formats, I address the format or obvious differences in a matter-of-fact manner, such as, "I have spiced things up with this menu and have three different ones that I will pass out. You may receive one that is different than your neighbor's but whichever one you receive is going to be lots of fun for you!" Other times, when the menus are very similar in their format and graphics, I just distribute them and address concerns when they are brought up. For the most part, students are more likely to simply go with what they have been given when any differences in menus are presented confidently without being open to debate or complaint.

CHAPTER 3

Guidelines for Products

". . . each project is unique."

—Fifth-grade student, when asked why he enjoys choice menus

This chapter outlines the different types of products used in the featured menus, as well as the guidelines and expectations for each. It is very important that students understand the expectations of a completed product before they choose to work on it. By discussing these expectations before students begin and having the information readily available at the time of product selection, you will limit the frustration on everyone's part.

$1 Contract

> *"I really appreciate the $1 form. It kept me from having to run to [craft store] and spend $60 on felt and glitter and all of the other things we normally have to buy for projects."*
>
> —Parent of one of my students when asked
> for feedback on a recent menu

Consideration should be given to the cost of creating the products included on any menu. The resources available to students vary within a classroom, and students should not be graded on the amount of materials they can purchase to make a product look better. These menus are designed to equalize the resources students have available. The materials for most products are available for less than a dollar and can often be found in a teacher's classroom as part of the classroom supplies. If a product requires materials from the student, a $1 contract is noted as part of the product's guidelines. This is a very important in the explanation of the product. First of all, by limiting the amount of money a child can spend, it creates an equal amount of resources for all students. Second, it actually encourages a more creative product; when students are limited by the amount of materials they can readily purchase, they often have to use materials from home in new and unique ways. Figure 3.1 is a sample of the contract that has been used many times in my classroom with various products.

$1 Contract

I did not spend more than $1.00 on my _____.

_____ _____
           Student Signature   Date

My child, _____, did not spend more than $1.00 on the product he or she created.

_____ _____
           Parent Signature   Date

Figure 3.1. $1 contract.

The Products

Table 3.1 contains a list of the products used in this book. These products were chosen for their flexibility in addressing various learning styles as well as being popular products most students have experienced; teachers may already be using these in their classroom, which makes the product easy for the students to understand. The products have been sorted by learning style—visual, kinesthetic, or auditory. Each menu has been designed to include products from all of the learning styles. Some of the products may fit into more than one area depending on how they are presented or implemented (and some of the best products cross over between styles), but you will find them listed by their most common application. The specific guidelines for all of the products are presented in an easy-to-read card format (see the section on Product Guidelines), which can be reproduced for students. This format is convenient for students to have in front of them when they work on their products.

Product Frustrations

One of the biggest frustrations that accompanies the use of various products on menus is the barrage of questions about the products themselves. Students can become so wrapped up in the products and the criteria for creating them that they do not focus on the content being presented. This is especially true when menus are first introduced to the class. Students can spend an exorbitant amount of time asking the teacher about the products mentioned on the menu. When this happens, what should have been a 10–15 minute menu introduction turns into 45–50 minutes of discussion about product expectations. Most teachers cannot afford to spend even a little time discussing the attributes of a PowerPoint presentation when there is content to be discussed.

Another frustration often comes when showing students product examples. In order to facilitate the introduction of the menu products, teachers may consider showing their students examples of the product(s) from the previous year. Although this can be helpful, it can also lead to additional frustration on the part of both the teacher and the student. Some students may not feel they can produce a product as nice, big, special, or (you fill in the blank) as the example, or when shown an example, take that to mean the teacher would like something exactly like the one they are shown. To avoid this situation, I would propose that, if using examples, the example students are shown be a "blank" example that demonstrates how to create the shell of the product. If an example of a window-pane is needed, for example, then students might be shown a blank piece of paper

Table 3.1

Products

Visual/Written	Kinesthetic	Verbal/Auditory
Acrostic	Board Game	Children's Book
Advertisement	Book Cover	Commercial
Book Cover	Bulletin Board Display	Interview
Brochure/Pamphlet	Collage	News Report
Bulletin Board Display	Commercial	Play
Bumper Sticker	Concentration Cards	Presentation of Created
Cartoon/Comic Strip	Costume	Product
Children's Book	Diorama	Power Point–Speaker
Collage	Folded Quiz Book	Puppet
Crossword Puzzle	Flipbook	Speech
Drawing	Mask	Song/Rap
Diary/Journal	Mobile	Student-Taught Lesson
Folded Quiz Book	Model	You Be the Person
Greeting Card	Mural	Presentation
Instruction Card	Play	Video
Letter	Puppet	
Map	Product Cube	
Mind Map	Quiz Board	
Newspaper Article	Scrapbook	
Picture Dictionary	Student-Taught Lesson	
Poster	Three-Dimensional	
Power Point–Stand	Timeline	
Alone	Trading Cards	
Questionnaire	Trophy	
Quiz Board	Video	
Recipe		
Scrapbook		
Story		
Trading Cards		
Three Facts and a Fib		
Venn Diagram		
Window Pane		
Worksheet		

that is divided into six panes. The students can then take the "skeleton" of the product and make it their own as they create their own version of the windowpane using their information.

Product Guidelines

"Wow. You know how great these are . . . how much time they will save?"

—A group of teachers, when presented with a page of products guidelines for their classroom

Most frustrations associated with products can be addressed proactively through the use of standardized, predetermined product guidelines that are shared with students prior to their selecting and subsequently creating any products. These product guidelines are designed in a specific yet generic way, such that anytime throughout the school year that the students select a product, its guidelines will apply. A beneficial side effect of using set guidelines for a product is the security it creates. Students are often reticent to try something new as it requires taking a risk on their part. Traditionally, when students select products, they ask questions about creating it; hope they remember and understood all of the details and turn it in. It can be quite a surprise when they receive the product back and realize that it was not complete, or did not meet the teacher's expectations. As you can imagine, students may not want to take the risk on something new the next time; they would prefer to do what they know and be successful. Through the use of product guidelines, students can begin to feel secure in their choice of product before they start working on the product itself. If they are not feeling secure, they tend to stay within their comfort zone.

The product guidelines for all of the menu products, as well as some potential free-choice options, are included in an easy-to-read card format (see Figure 3.2) with a graphic that depicts the guidelines and helps the students remember the important criteria for each product. (The guidelines for some products, such as summaries, are omitted because teachers often have different criteria for these products.) Once the products and/or menus have been selected, there are many options available to share this information.

Sharing Product Guidelines With Students

There really is no one "right way" to share the product guideline information with your students. It all depends on their abilities and needs. Some teachers choose to duplicate and distribute all of the product guideline pages to students at the beginning of the year so each child has his own copy in front of him while he works on his products. As another option, a few classroom sets can be created by gluing each product guideline onto separate index cards, hole punching the corner of each card, and placing them on a metal ring. These ring sets can be placed in a central location, or at a center where students can borrow and return them as they work on their products. Using a ring also allows for the addition of new products as they are introduced to the whole class or through future menus. Some teachers prefer to introduce product guidelines as students experience them on their menus. In this case, product guidelines from the menu currently assigned can be enlarged, laminated, and posted on a bulletin board for easy access during classroom work time. Some teachers may choose to reproduce each menu's specific product guidelines on the back of the menu. No matter which method a teacher chooses to share the information with the students, he or she will save a lot of time and frustration by having the product guidelines available for student reference (e.g., "Look at your product guidelines, I think that will answer your question.")

Story Map

One of the most commonly used products in a language arts classroom is the story map. The story map is a quick and effective way for a student to dissect a story and show that he or she can analyze the important parts of the story. Story maps are an option for many of the menus provided in this book, and I advise teachers to use the story map they prefer. Three examples are offered (see Figures 3.3, 3.4, and 3.5) and each are coded to match the levels found in the tiered menus; however, teachers who have a favorite format that students are accustomed to should feel free to use their own.

Write the word
Oval letters
Remember the word
Draw a picture

Acrostic

- At least 8.5" x 11"
- Neatly written or typed
- Target word will be written down the left side of the paper
- Each descriptive word chosen must begin with one of the letters from the target word
- Each descriptive word chosen must be related to the target word

Information

$8.00

Nice, White Shirt

Advertisement

- At least 8.5" x 11"
- Should include a slogan
- Color picture of item or service
- Include price, if appropriate

Book Cover

- Front Cover–title, author, image
- Cover Inside Flap–summary of book
- Back Inside Flap–brief biography of author
- Back Cover–comments about book
- Spine–title and author
- May be placed on actual book, but does not have to be

Brochure/Pamphlet

- At least 8.5" x 11"
- Must be in three-fold format; front fold has title and picture
- Must have both pictures and information
- Information should be in paragraph form with at least five facts included

Figure 3.2. Product guidelines.

Bulletin Board Display

- Must fit within assigned space
- Should include at least 10 facts
- Must have a title
- Must share information in different ways

Bumper Sticker

- Uses a regular piece of paper cut in half lengthwise
- Must have a picture to meet the task
- Must have a motto

Cartoon/Comic Strip

- At least 8.5" x 11"
- At least six cells
- Must have meaningful dialogue
- Must have color

Children's Book

- Must have cover with book's title and author's name
- Must have at least five pages
- Each page should have an illustration to accompany the story
- Should be neatly written or typed
- Can be developed on the computer

Figure 3.2. Continued.

Collage

- At least 8.5" x 11"
- Pictures must be neatly cut from magazines or newspapers (no clip art)
- Label items as required in task

Commercial

- Must be between 2–3 minutes
- Script must be turned in before commercial is presented
- Can be presented live to an audience or recorded
- Should have props or some form of costume
- Can include more than one person

Concentration Cards

- At least 20 index cards (10 matching sets)
- Can use both pictures and words
- Information should be placed on just one side of each card
- Include an answer key that shows the matches
- All cards must be submitted in a carrying bag

Crossword Puzzle

- Must include at least 20 significant words or phrases
- Clues must be appropriate
- Include puzzle and answer key

Figure 3.2. Continued.

Diary

- Neatly written or typed
- Include appropriate number of entries
- Include date, if appropriate
- Must be written in first person

Dictionary

- Neatly written or made on the computer
- Definition should be in students's own words
- Has a clear picture for each word
- Pictures can be drawn or from the computer

Diorama

- At least 4" x 5" x 8"
- Must be self-standing
- All interior space covered with relevant pictures and information
- Name written on back in permanent ink
- $1 contract signed
- Informational/title card attached to diorama

Drawing

- Must be at least 8.5" x 11"
- Must include color
- Must be neatly drawn by hand
- Must have title
- Name should be written on the back

Figure 3.2. Continued.

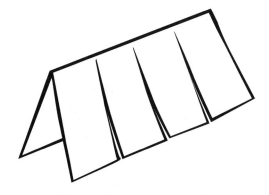

Flipbook

- At least 8.5" x 11" folded in half
- All information or opinions must be supported by facts
- Created with the correct number of flaps cut into top
- Color is optional
- Name written on the back

Game

- At least four thematic game pieces
- At least 25 colored/thematic squares
- At least 20 question/activity cards
- A thematic title on the board
- A complete set of rules for playing the game
- At least the size of an open file folder

Greeting Card

- Front–colored pictures, words optional
- Front Inside–personal note related to topic
- Back Inside–greeting or saying, must meet product criteria
- Back Outside–logo, publisher, and price for card

Instruction Card

- Created on heavy paper or card
- Neatly written or typed
- Uses color drawings
- Provides instructions stated

Figure 3.2. Continued.

Interview

- Must have at least five questions important to topic being studied
- Questions and answers must be neatly written or typed
- Must include name of person being interviewed
- Must get teacher or parent permission before interviewing person

Letter

- Neatly written or typed
- Must use proper letter format
- At least three paragraphs
- Must follow type of letter stated in menu (friendly, persuasive, informational)

List

- Neatly written or made on the computer
- Has the number of items required
- Is as complete as possible
- Alphabet lists need words or phrases for each letter of the alphabet except X

Map

- At least 8.5" x 11"
- Accurate information
- Must include at least 10 relevant locations
- Includes compass rose, legend, scale, key

Figure 3.2. Continued.

Mask

- Can be worn over your face
- Should be able to see with it on the face
- Can be easily attached and removed from your head
- $1 contract signed

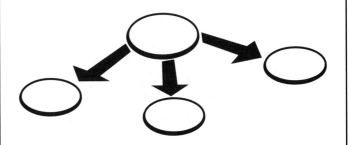

Mind Map

- At least 8.5" x 11" unlined paper
- Must have one central idea
- Follow the "no more than four rule" (there should be no more than four words coming from any one word)

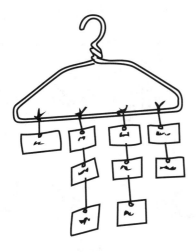

Mobile

- At least 10 pieces of related information
- Includes color and pictures
- At least three layers of hanging information
- Be able to hang in a balanced way

Model

- At least 8" x 8" x 12"
- Parts of model must be labeled
- Should be to scale when appropriate
- Must include a title card
- Name permanently written on model
- $1 contract signed

Figure 3.2. Continued.

Mural

- Should be the size of a poster board or larger
- Include at least five pieces of information
- Should use different colors
- May include words; must have a title
- Write your name on the back

News Report

- Must address the who, what, where, when, why, and how of topic
- Script of report turned in with project (or before if performance will be live)
- Can be either live or recorded

Newspaper Article

- Must be informational in nature
- Must follow standard newspaper format
- Must include picture with caption that supports article
- At least three paragraphs
- Neatly written or typed

Play

- Must be between 3–5 minutes
- Script must be turned in before play is presented
- Must be presented to an audience
- Should have props or some form of costume
- Can include more than one person

Figure 3.2. Continued.

Poster

- Should be size of standard poster board
- At least five pieces of important information
- Must have title
- Must have both words and pictures
- Name must be written on back

PowerPoint — Speaker

- At least 10 informational slides and one title slide with student's name
- No more than two words per page
- Slides must have color and at least one graphic per page
- Animations are optional but should not distract from information being presented
- Presentation should be timed and flow with speech being given

PowerPoint — Stand-Alone

- At least 10 informational slides and one title slide with student's name
- No more than 10 words per page
- Slides must have color and at least one graphic per page
- Animations are optional but must not distract from information being presented

Product Cube

- All six sides of cube must be filled with information
- Name must be printed neatly on bottom of one side of cube

Figure 3.2. Continued.

Puppet

- Puppet must be handmade and must have a moveable mouth
- A list of supplies used to make puppet must be turned in with puppet
- $1 contract signed
- If used in puppet show, all puppet show criteria must also be met

Puppet Show

- Must be between 3–5 minutes
- Script must be turned in before show is presented
- Must be presented to an audience
- Should have a different puppet for each role

Questionnaire

- Neatly written or typed
- At least 10 questions with possible answers
- At least one answer that requires a written response
- Questions must be related to topic being studied

Recipe/Recipe Card

- Must be written neatly or typed on a piece of paper or index card
- Must have list of ingredients with measurements for each
- Must have numbered steps that explain how to make the recipe

Figure 3.2. Continued.

Report

- Neatly written or made on the computer
- Must have enough information to address topic
- Information has to be student's own words, not copied from a book or the Internet

Scrapbook

- Cover of scrapbook must have meaningful title and student's name
- Must have at least five themed pages
- Each page must have at least one picture
- All photos must have captions

Sculpture

- Cannot be larger than 2 feet tall
- Must include any specified items
- Name should be written on bottom
- Must not use any valuable materials
- $1 contract signed

Song/Rap

- Words must make sense
- Can be presented to an audience or recorded
- Written words will be turned in
- Should be at least 1 minute in length

Figure 3.2. Continued.

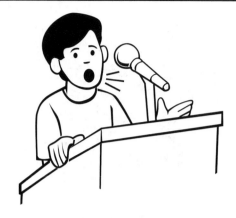

Speech

- Must be at least 2 minutes in length
- Should not be read from written paper
- Note cards can be used
- Written speech must be turned in
- Voice must be clear, loud, and easy to understand

Story

- Must be neatly written or typed
- Must have all elements of a well-written story (setting, characters, problem, events, resolution)
- Must be appropriate length to allow for story elements

Three Facts and a Fib

- Can be written, typed, or created using Microsoft PowerPoint
- Must include exactly four statements: three true statements and one false statement
- False statement should not obvious
- Brief paragraph should be included that explains why the fib is false

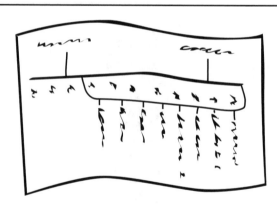

Timeline

- No bigger than standard-sized poster board
- Must be divided into equal intervals of time
- Must contain at least 10 important dates
- Must have an explanation of at least two sentences for each date about its importance

Figure 3.2. Continued.

Trading Cards

- Include at least 10 cards
- Each card should be at least 3" x 5"
- Each should have a colored picture
- At least three facts on the subject of the card
- Cards must have information on both sides
- All cards must be submitted in a carrying bag

Trophy

- Must be at least 6 inches tall
- Must have a base with the winner's name and the name of the award written neatly or typed on it
- Top of trophy must be appropriate to the award
- Name should be written on the bottom of the award
- Must be an originally designed trophy (avoid reusing a trophy from home)

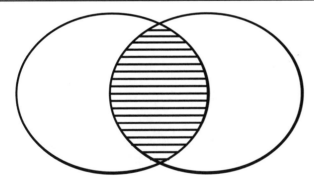

Venn Diagram

- At least 8.5" x 11"
- Shapes should be thematic and neatly drawn
- Must have a title for entire diagram and a title for each section
- Must have at least six items in each section of diagram
- Name must be written on back

Video

- Must be recorded
- Must turn in written plan or storyboard with project
- Student must arrange to use own video recorder or allow teacher at least 3 days' notice for use of recorder
- Must cover important information about the project
- Name must be written on video or disc

Figure 3.2. Continued.

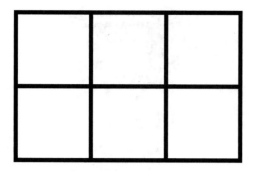

Windowpane

- At least 8.5" x 11" unlined paper
- At least six squares
- Each square must include a picture and words
- Name should be recorded on bottom right-hand corner of front

Worksheet

- Must be 8.5" x 11"
- Neatly written or typed
- Must cover specific topic or question in detail
- Must be creative in design
- Must have at least one graphic
- Must turn in corresponding answer key

You Be the Person Presentation

- Take on the role of the person
- Cover at least five important facts about the life of the person
- Should be between 2–4 minutes in length
- Script must be turned in before information is presented
- Should present to an audience and answer questions while staying in character
- Must have props or some form of costume

Figure 3.2. Continued.

Title: _____

_____

Author: _____

Illustrator: _____

Setting of Story

_____

_____

_____

_____

_____

_____

Characters in Story

Write each character's name and give a description of the character.

_____

_____

_____

_____

Events in Story

Write all of the important events in the story, in order.

_____

_____

_____

_____

_____

Figure 3.3. Story map 1.

© Prufrock Press Inc. • *Literature for Every Learner* • *Grades 3–5*

Permission is granted to photocopy or reproduce this page for single classroom use only.

47

Story Map

Title and Author	Setting

Main Characters
Write at least three traits for each character.

Supporting Characters
Write one sentence about why each is important to the story.

Problem

Major Events

Solution

Figure 3.4. Story map 2.

Story Map

Title and Author

Setting

Main Characters
Write at least three quotes from the text to show their traits.

Plot

Theme
Write quotes from the story to show this theme.

Figure 3.5. Story map 3.

CHAPTER 4

Rubrics

"All the grading of the projects kept me from using menus before. The rubric makes it easier though and they [the different projects] are fun to see."

—Fourth-grade teacher, when asked to explain reservations about using menus

The most common reason teachers feel uncomfortable with menus is the need for equality in grading. Teachers often feel it is easier to grade identical products created by all of the students, rather than grading a large number of different products, none of which looks like any other. The great equalizer for a multitude of different products is a generic rubric that can cover all of the important qualities of an excellent product.

All-Purpose Rubric

Figure 4.1 is an example of a rubric that has been classroom tested with various menus. This rubric can be used with any point value activity presented in a menu, as there are five criteria and the columns represent full points, half points, or no points. Although Tic-Tac-Toe, Three Shape, and Meal menus are not point based, this rubric can be used to grade products from these menus. Teachers simply assign 100 points to each of the products students select and then use the all-purpose rubric to grade each product individually based on a total of 100 points.

There are different ways that this rubric can be shared with students. Some teachers prefer to provide it when a menu is presented to students. This rubric can be reproduced on the back of the menu along with its guidelines. The rubric can also be given to students to keep in their folder with their product guideline cards so they always know the expectations as they complete products throughout the school year. Some teachers prefer to keep a master copy for themselves and post an enlarged copy of the rubric on a bulletin board, or provide one copy for parents during open house so they understand how their children's menu products will be graded.

No matter how the rubric is shared with students, the first time they see this rubric, it should be explained in detail, especially the last column titled "Self." It is very important that students self-evaluate their products. This column can provide a unique perspective of the project as it is being graded. *Note:* This rubric was designed to be specific enough that students will know the criteria the teacher is seeking, but general enough that they can still be as creative as they like in the creation of their product.

Student-Taught Lessons and Student Presentation Rubrics

Although the all-purpose rubric can be used for all activities, there are two occasions that seem to warrant a special rubric: student-taught lessons and student presentations. These are unique situations, with many details that must be considered to create a quality product.

Teachers often would like to allow students to teach their fellow classmates, but are concerned about quality lessons and may not be comfortable with the grading aspect of the assignment; rarely do students understand all of the components that go into designing an effective lesson. This student-taught lesson rubric helps focus the student on the important aspects of a well-designed lesson, and allows teachers to make the evaluation process a little more subjective. The student-taught lesson rubric (see Figure 4.2) included for these menus is appropriate for all levels.

Student presentations can be difficult to evaluate. The first consideration with these types of presentations is that of objectivity. The objectivity can be

Name: _____

All-Purpose Product Rubric

	Excellent (Full Points)	Good (Half Points)	Poor (No Points)	Self
Completeness Is everything included in the product?	All information needed is included. Meets product guidelines.	Some important information is missing. Meets product guidelines.	Most important information is missing or does not meet guidelines.	
Creativity Is the product original?	Information is creative. Graphics are original. Presentations are unique.	Information is creative. Graphics are not original or were found on the computer.	There is no evidence of new thoughts or perspectives in the product.	
Correctness Is all the information included correct?	All information in the product is correct.	Not applicable.	Any portion of the information included is incorrect.	
Appropriate Communication Is the information well communicated?	All information is neat, easy to read, or—if presented— easy to understand.	Most of the product is neat, easy to read, and—if presented— easy to understand.	The product is not neat or is not easy to read.	
Effort and Time Did student put significant effort into the product?	Effort is obvious.	Not applicable.	The product does not show significant effort.	

Figure 4.1. All-purpose product rubric.

Name: _____

Student-Taught Lesson Grading Rubric

Parts of Lesson	Excellent	Good	Fair	Poor	Self
Prepared and Ready: All materials and lesson ready at start of class period, from warm-up to conclusion of lesson.	10 Everything is ready to present.	6 Lesson is present, but small amount of scrambling.	3 Lesson is present, but major scrambling.	0 No lesson ready or missing major components.	
Understanding: Presenter understands the material well. Students understand information presented.	20 Presenter understands; almost all of the students understand information.	12 Presenter understands; 25% of students do not.	4 Presenter understands; 50% of students do not.	0 Presenter is confused.	
Completion: Includes all significant information from section or topic.	15 Includes all important information.	10 Includes most important information.	2 Includes less than 50% of the important information.	0 Information is not related.	
Practice: Includes some way for students to practice or access the information.	20 Practice present, well chosen.	10 Practice present, can be applied effectively.	5 Practice present, not related or best choice.	0 No practice or students are confused.	
Interest/Fun: Most of the class is involved, interested, and participating.	15 Everyone interested and participating.	10 75% actively participating.	5 Less than 50% actively participating.	0 Everyone off task.	
Creativity: Information presented in an imaginative way.	20 Wow, creative! I never would have thought of that!	12 Good ideas!	5 Some good pieces but general instruction.	0 No creativity; all lecture/ notes/ worksheet.	
				Total Grade:	

Your Topic/Objective:

Comments:

Don't Forget:

All copy requests and material requests must be made at least 24 hours in advance.

Figure 4.2. Student-taught lesson grading rubric.

addressed through a very specific presentation rubric that reinforces the expectations for the speaker. The rubric will need to be discussed and various criteria demonstrated before the students begin preparing their presentations. The second consideration is that of the audience and its interest in the presentation. How frustrating is it to have to grade 30 presentations when the audience is not paying attention, off task, or tuning out? This can be solved by allowing your audience to be directly involved in the presentation by presenting them with a rubric that can be used to provide feedback to their classmates. If all of the students have been instructed on the student presentation rubric (see Figure 4.3) when they receive their feedback rubric, then they will be quite comfortable with the criteria. Students are asked to rank their classmates on a scale of 1–10 in the areas of content, flow, and the prop they chose to enhance their presentation (see Figure 4.4). Students are also asked to state two things the presenter did well. Although most students understand this should be a positive experience for the presenter, it may need to be reinforced that certain types of feedback are not necessary; for example, if the presenter dropped her prop and had to pick it up, the presenter knows this and it probably does not need to be noted again. The feedback should be positive and specific, as well. A comment of "Great!" is not what should be recorded; instead, something specific such as, "You spoke loudly and clearly" or "You had great drawings!" should be written on the form. These types of comments really make the students take note and feel great about their presentations. The teacher should not be surprised to note that the students often look through all of their classmates' feedback and comments before ever consulting the rubric the teacher completed. Once students have completed a feedback form for a presenter, the forms can then be gathered at the end of each presentation, stapled together, and given to the presenter at the end of the class.

Name: _____

Student Presentation Rubric

	Excellent	Good	Fair	Poor	Self
Content Complete Did the presentation include everything it should?	**30** Presentation included all important information about topic being presented.	**20** Presentation covered most of the important information, but one key idea was missing.	**10** Presentation covered some of the important information, but more than one key idea was missing.	**0** Presentation covered information, but the information was trivial or fluff.	
Content Correct Was the information presented accurate?	**30** All information presented was accurate.	**20** All information presented was correct, with a few unintentional errors that were quickly corrected.	Not applicable: There is no middle ground when it comes to correctness of content.	**0** Any information presented was not correct.	
Prop Did the speaker have at least one prop that was directly related to the presentation?	**20** Presenter had a prop and it complemented the presentation.	**12** Presenter had a prop, but it was not the best choice.	**4** Presenter had a prop, but there was no clear reason for it.	**0** Presenter had no prop.	
Content Consistent Did the speaker stay on topic?	**10** Presenter stayed on topic 100% of the time.	**7** Presenter stayed on topic 90–99% of the time.	**4** Presenter stayed on topic 80–89% of the time.	**0** It was hard to tell what the topic was.	
Flow Was the speaker familiar and comfortable with the material so that it flowed well?	**10** Presentation flowed well. Speaker did not stumble over words.	**7** Presenter had some flow problems, but they did not distract from information.	**4** Some flow problems interrupted the presentation, and presenter seemed flustered.	**0** Constant flow problems occurred, and information was not presented so that it could be understood.	
				Total Grade:	

Figure 4.3. Student presentation rubric.

Topic: _____   **Student's Name:**_____

On a scale of 1–10, rate the following areas:

Content (How in depth was the information? How well did the speaker know the information? Was the information correct? Could the speaker answer questions?)		Give one short reason why you gave this number.
Flow (Did the presentation flow smoothly? Did the speaker appear confident and ready to speak?)		Give one short reason why you gave this number.
Prop (Did the speaker explain his or her prop? Did this choice seem logical? Was it the best choice?)		Give one short reason why you gave this number.

Comments: Below, write two things that you think the presenter did well:

1. _____

_____

2. _____

_____

- -

Topic: _____   **Student's Name:**_____

On a scale of 1–10, rate the following areas:

Content (How in depth was the information? How well did the speaker know the information? Was the information correct? Could the speaker answer questions?)		Give one short reason why you gave this number.
Flow (Did the presentation flow smoothly? Did the speaker appear confident and ready to speak?)		Give one short reason why you gave this number.
Prop (Did the speaker explain his or her prop? Did this choice seem logical? Was it the best choice?)		Give one short reason why you gave this number.

Comments: Below, write two things that you think the presenter did well:

1. _____

_____

2. _____

_____

Figure 4.4. Student feedback form.

The Menus

The stories, novels, and poems that have been selected for inclusion in this book are found on the list of text exemplars in Appendix B of the Common Core State Standards for English Language Arts, which can be accessed at http://www.corestandards.org/assets/Appendix_B.pdf.

How to Use the Menu Pages

Each menu in this section has:
- an introduction page for the teacher;
- a highly modified menu, indicated by a triangle (▲) in the upper right hand corner;
- a moderately modified menu, indicated by a circle (●) in the upper right hand corner
- an unmodified, advanced menu, indicated by a square (■) in the upper right hand corner and,
- any specific activities mentioned on the menus.

Introduction Pages

The introduction pages are meant to provide an overview of each menu. They are divided into various areas.

1. *Title and Menu Type.* The top of each introductory page will note the title of the story, novel, or poem as well as the menu type(s) used. Each novel included has three menus, a highly modified menu (▲), a slightly modified/on-level menu (●), and an advanced menu (■). When possible, all three menus are in the same format, however, sometimes in order to modify for special needs students, the lowest level menu may have a different format to control the amount of choice a student faces at one time. The Poetry Shape menus cover all three levels within one menu.

2. *Brief Synopsis.* Under the title of the menu, a brief synopsis of the text has been included for teacher reference.

3. *Objectives Covered Through the Menu and Activities.* This area will list all of the objectives that the menu can address. Menus are arranged in such a way that if students complete the guidelines set forth in the menu's instructions, all of these objectives will be covered. Some objectives may be designated with a shape at the end, which indicates that the specific objective is only addressed on its corresponding menu.

4. *Materials Needed by Students for Completion.* The introduction page includes a list of materials that may be needed by students as they complete either menu. Any materials listed that are used in only **one** of the three menus are designated with that menu's corresponding shape code. Students do have the choice in the menu items they would like to complete, so it is possible that the teacher will not need all of these materials for every student. In addition to any materials listed for specific menus, it is expected that the teacher will provide, or students will have access to, the following materials for each menu:
   a. lined paper;
   b. blank 8.5" x 11" white paper;
   c. glue; and
   d. crayons, colored pencils, or markers.

5. *Special Notes on the Modifications of These Menus.* Some menu formats have special management issues or considerations when it comes to modifying for different ability levels. This section will review additional options available for modifying each menu.

6. *Special Notes on the Use of This Menu.* Some menus allow students to present demonstrations, experiments, songs, or PowerPoint presentations to their classmates. This section will provide any special tips on managing

products that may require more time, supplies, or space. This section will also share any tips to consider for a specific activity.

7. *Time Frame.* Each menu has its own ideal time frame based on its structure, but all work best with at least a one-week time frame. Menus that assess more objectives are better suited to more than 2 weeks. This section will give you an overview about the best time frame for completing the entire menu, as well as options for shorter time periods. If teachers do not have time to devote to an entire menu, they certainly can choose the 1–2-day option for any menu topic students are currently studying.

8. *Suggested Forms.* This is a list of the rubrics, templates, or reproducibles that should be available for students as the menus are introduced and completed. If a menu has a free-choice option, the appropriate proposal form also will be listed here.

CHAPTER 5

Novels and Short Stories

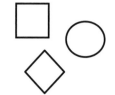

The Stories
Julian Tells

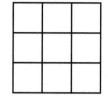

Three Shape Menu ▲
and Tic-Tac-Toe Menu ● ■

Julian has a very creative imagination that sometimes gets him in trouble. In this six-chapter book, he eats too much pudding, convinces his brother Huey that catalogs bring cats, develops his own way to grow taller, plants a unique garden, deals with a loose tooth, and makes a new friend.

Reading Objectives Covered Through These Menus and These Activities

- Students will interpret figurative language and multiple meaning words.
- Students will make and explain inferences made from the story.
- Students will show comprehension by retelling or acting out events in a story.
- Students will show comprehension by summarizing a story.
- Students will analyze characters, their relationships, and their importance in the story.

Writing Objectives Covered Through These Menus and These Activities

- Students will write to express their feelings, reflect, inform, explain, describe, entertain, or narrate.

Materials Needed by Students for Completion

- *The Stories Julian Tells* by Ann Cameron
- Blank index cards (for trading cards)
- Magazines (for collages) ▲
- Seed catalog
- Scrapbooking materials
- Large lined index cards (for instruction cards ▲, recipe cards ■)
- DVD or VHS recorder (for how-to video) ● ■
- Ruler (for comic strip) ●

Special Notes on the Modifications of These Menus

- This topic has two different menu formats: Three Shape menu (▲) and Tic-Tac-Toe (● ■) menu. The Three Shape menu is specifically selected for the triangle option, as it easily allows the menu to be broken into manageable bits; the three shapes visually separate the page, making it less daunting for special needs students. The space between the three shapes makes it easy for the teacher to cut the menu as needed based on the comfort level of the students. If it is the first time choice is being introduced, then the children may receive only the strip of the top row (or square) options. Then, when they have finished one of those options, they can receive a strip of circles and finally, the enrichment-level diamond activities. After students have grown more accustomed to making choices, the menu might be cut just once after the circles, so students can select a square and a circle and submit them to the teacher. Then, they can choose from the diamond strip they receive. The ultimate goal would be for students to have all nine options at once and not be overwhelmed.

Special Notes on the Use of These Menus

- These menus give students the opportunity to create a video. Although students enjoy producing their own videos, there often are difficulties obtaining the equipment and scheduling the use of a video recorder. This activity can be modified by allowing students to act out the video (like a play) or, if students have the technology, allowing them to produce a webcam version of their product.

Time Frame

- 1–3 weeks—Students are given a menu as the story or novel is started. As reading progresses and the teacher presents lessons throughout the week, he or she should refer back to the menu options associated with that content. The teacher will go over all of the options for the story and have students indicate the activities they are most interested in completing. When using the Tic-Tac-Toe format, students should complete a column or a row. If they are using the Three Shape format, students will be complete an activity for each of the three shapes. When students complete these patterns, they have completed one activity from each content area, learning style, or level of Bloom's revised taxonomy, depending on the design of the menu.
- 1 week—At the start of the unit, the teacher chooses the three activities he or she feels are most valuable for students. Stations can be set up in the classroom. These three activities are available for student choice throughout the week as regular instruction takes place.
- 1–2 days—The teacher chooses an activity from the menus to use with the entire class.

Suggested Forms

- All-purpose rubric
- Student presentation rubric
- Free-choice proposal form

The Stories Julian Tells

Directions: Circle one choice from each group of shapes. Color in the shape after you have finished it. All products are due by : _____.

Julian's father really liked making pudding. Create a picture dictionary of at least eight different terms used in cooking, including beating and whipping.

Make a collage of at least 10 words that have multiple meanings (like beating) or fun associations (like *cat*-alog).

Create a set of trading cards for four of the dozen cats that might have answered Huey's request. Each cat should have special skills that make it qualified to work in their garden.

Pretend you are going to plant your own garden. Using a seed catalog, choose a type of seed you would like to plant. Write a paragraph about why you would to plant this seed.

Design a cartoon about a child who does something funny in order to grow taller.

Julian's father gave him different ways to take out his loose tooth. Ask your classmates which way they thought was best and make a poster to show your findings.

Write an acrostic for the word *friendship*. Use ideas from the book for each letter.

Write an instruction card for making and flying a wish kite.

Create a wish scrapbook with five different pages. Put a special wish on each page.

The Stories Julian Tells

Directions: Check the boxes you plan to complete. They should form a tic-tac-toe across or down. All activities must be completed by : _____.

☐ **"Gloria Who Might Be My Best Friend"**	☐ **"The Pudding Like a Night on the Sea"**	☐ **"Catalog Cats"**
Create a best friend greeting card that you could give to Gloria after you fly your wish kite.	Julian's father really liked making pudding. Create a picture dictionary of different terms used in cooking, including beating and whipping.	It made sense to Huey that cats might come from catalogs since the word *catalog* begins with *cat*. Design an advertisement for another animal that might come from a creative place based on its name.
☐ **"My Very Strange Teeth"**	☐ **Free Choice: "Gloria Who Might Be My Best Friend"** (Fill out your proposal form before beginning the free choice!)	☐ **"Our Garden"**
Julian's father gave him a few different ways to take out his loose tooth. Record a video that shows different ways someone could remove a loose tooth.		Pretend you are going to plant your own garden. Using a seed catalog, choose a type of seed you would like to plant. Create a poster that tells about this plant and why you think it would be perfect for your garden.
☐ **"Because of Figs"**	☐ **"Catalog Cats"**	☐ **"Gloria Who Might Be My Best Friend"**
Design a comic strip about a child who does something funny in order to grow taller.	Create a set of trading cards for six of the dozen cats that might have answered Huey's request. Each cat should have special skills that make it qualified to work in their garden.	Create a wish scrapbook with five different pages. Put a special wish on each page.

The Stories Julian Tells

Directions: Check the boxes you plan to complete. They should form a tic-tac-toe across or down. All activities must be completed by : _____.

☐ **"Gloria Who Might Be My Best Friend"** Create two best friend greeting cards: one card Julian could give Gloria after they fly their wish kite, the other Gloria could give to Julian sharing her two wishes.	☐ **"The Pudding Like a Night on the Sea"** Julian's father really liked making pudding. Write a recipe card for something you like to make, and if possible, make it for your classmates.	☐ **"Catalog Cats"** It made sense to Huey that cats might come from catalogs since the word *catalog* begins with *cat*. Design an advertisement for another thing or animal that might come from a creative place based on its name.
☐ **"My Very Strange Teeth"** Julian's father gave him a few different ways to take out his loose tooth. Record a video that shares all of the different ways someone could remove a loose tooth and which method you recommend.	☐ **Free Choice: "Gloria Who Might Be My Best Friend"** (Fill out your proposal form before beginning the free choice!)	☐ **"Our Garden"** Pretend you are going to plant your own garden. Using a seed catalog, choose two plants you would like to plant. Write a letter to your parents explaining why you would like a garden and why these two plants should be planted in it.
☐ **"Because of Figs"** Write your own children's book about a child who wants to grow taller and the different things he or she does in order to grow.	☐ **"Catalog Cats"** Create a set of trading cards for the dozen cats that might have answered Huey's request. Each cat should have special skills that make it qualified to work in their garden.	☐ **"Gloria Who Might Be My Best Friend"** Create a wish scrapbook with seven different pages. Put one of your special wishes on each page.

Tops and Bottoms

2-5-8 Menus

In this folktale, Hare strikes a deal with Bear that if Bear allows him to plant a crop on his land, he will give him half of the crop. When offered a choice of the plants, Bear chooses tops, then bottoms, and then tops and bottoms. It seems, however, that Hare is quite tricky.

Reading Objectives Covered Through These Menus and These Activities

- Students will make predictions based on what is read.
- Students will show comprehension by retelling or acting out events in a story.
- Students will show comprehension by summarizing a story.
- Students will represent textual evidence by using story maps.
- Students will analyze characters, their relationships, and their importance in the story.
- Students will recognize and analyze story plot and problem resolution.

Writing Objectives Covered Through These Menus and These Activities

- Students will write to express their feelings, reflect, inform, explain, describe, entertain, or narrate.

Materials Needed by Students for Completion

- *Tops and Bottoms* by Janet Stevens
- Poster board or large white paper
- Coat hangers (for mobiles)
- String (for mobiles)
- Recycled materials (for diorama) ▲
- Story map ▲
- Socks (for puppets)
- DVD or VHS recorder (for commercials ● ■, news reports ■)
- Blank index cards (for mobiles)
- Aluminum foil (for quiz boards) ■
- Holiday lights (for quiz boards) ■
- Wires (for quiz boards) ■

Special Notes on the Modifications of These Menus

- If needed, further modifications can be made to a 2-5-8 menu based on the needs of your students. The easiest modification is altering the point goal from 10; lowering or raising the goal on a menu by one (or two) points is appropriate if additional modification up or down is needed.

Special Notes on the Use of These Menus

- The circle and square menus give students the opportunity to record a news report and commercial. Although students enjoy producing their own videos, there often are difficulties obtaining the equipment and scheduling the use of a video recorder. This activity can be modified by allowing students to act out the video (like a play) or, if students have the technology, allowing them to produce a webcam version of their product.
- These menus ask students to use recycled materials to create their diorama. This does not mean only plastic and paper; instead, students should focus on using materials in new ways. It works well if a box is started for "recycled" contributions at the beginning of the school year. That way, students always have access to these types of materials.
- The square ■ menu provides the opportunity for students to create a quiz board. A student friendly informational sheet that offers the steps for constructing their own quiz board is available at http://www.cesiscience.org/attachments/article/100/QuizBoardDirections.pdf.

Time Frame

- 1–2 weeks—Students are given a menu as the story is started, and the teacher discusses all of the product options on the menu. As the different options are discussed, students will choose the activities they are most interested in completing so they meet their goal of 10 points. As the reading progresses through the week(s), the teacher and students refer back to the menu options associated with the content being taught.
- 1–2 days—The teacher chooses an activity or product from the menus to use with the entire class.

Suggested Forms

- All-purpose rubric
- Student presentation rubric
- Proposal form for point-based projects

Tops and Bottoms

Directions: Choose at least two activities from the options below. The activities must total 10 points. Place a checkmark next to each box to show which activities you will complete. All activities must be completed by: _____.

---

2 Points

❑ Create a mobile with the tops, bottoms, and middles of the vegetables used in this story.

❑ Make a picture dictionary for all of the words in the story that were new to you.

---

5 Points

❑ Design a diorama for the most important scene in the story. Write a paragraph to explain why you picked this scene.

❑ This book opens up and down. Make a poster to show how this goes with the story.

❑ Complete a story map for *Tops and Bottoms*. Be sure to include information about the characters!

❑ Free choice: Submit a proposal form for a product of your choice.

---

8 Points

❑ Create a puppet for your favorite character in the story. Have the puppet retell what happened in the story.

❑ Choose another folktale or fable that has a trickster as a main character. Use a Venn diagram to compare the two stories.

Tops and Bottoms

Directions: Choose at least two activities from the options below. The activities must total 10 points. Place a checkmark next to each box to show which activities you will complete. All activities must be completed by: _____.

2 Points

☐ Create a mobile for at least two other tops, bottoms, and middles vegetables not used in this story.

☐ Make a picture dictionary for all of the words in the story that are related to money and business.

5 Points

☐ Choose another folktale or fable that has a trickster as a main character. Use a Venn diagram to compare the two stories.

☐ This book is made differently. Find at least two more books that are made differently and make a poster to share how their differences add to the story.

☐ Make a three-dimensional timeline for the events in the story. Include at least three events that happened before the story started.

☐ Free choice: Submit a proposal form for a product of your choice.

8 Points

☐ Create a puppet for your favorite character in the story. Have the puppet retell what happened in the story from his or her point of view.

☐ Make a commercial for the Hares' vegetable stand. Include what they sell and why someone would want to shop there.

Tops and Bottoms

Directions: Choose at least two activities from the options below. The activities must total 10 points. Place a checkmark next to each box to show which activities you will complete. All activities must be completed by: _____.

2 Points

❑ Create a mobile for at least three other tops, bottoms, and middles vegetables not used in this story.

❑ Make a quiz board to test your classmates on the definitions for all of the words in the story that are related to money and business.

5 Points

❑ Create a puppet for your favorite character in the story. Have the puppet retell what happened in the story from his or her point of view.

❑ Write and perform a song that the hare and his family may have sung while working in the garden.

❑ Make a commercial for the Hares' vegetable stand. Include what they sell and why someone would want to shop there.

❑ Free choice: Submit a proposal form for a product of your choice.

8 Points

❑ Perform a news report about the importance of understanding exactly what someone means before agreeing to a deal with him or her.

❑ Choose another folktale or fable that has a trickster as a main character. Compare the stories and then create your own children's book featuring this kind of character.

The Lighthouse Family: The Storm

2-5-8 Menus

After being saved as a kitten during a storm by a lighthouse beacon, Pandora decided to go to work as a lighthouse keeper. It was very lonely work, as most visitors simply passed by. After 4 years as a lighthouse keeper, her beacon, which may have saved many other lives, brings her a family.

Reading Objectives Covered Through These Menus and These Activities

- Students will make predictions based on what is read.
- Students will show comprehension by retelling or acting out events in a story.
- Students will show comprehension by summarizing a story.
- Students will represent textual evidence by using story maps.
- Students will analyze characters, their relationships, and their importance in the story.

Writing Objectives Covered Through These Menus and These Activities

- Students will write to express their feelings, reflect, inform, explain, describe, entertain, or narrate.

Materials Needed by Students for Completion

- *The Lighthouse Family: The Storm* by Cynthia Rylant
- Poster board or large white paper
- Recycled materials (for trophies, models ●)
- Magazines (for collages) ▲ ■
- Story map
- Socks (for puppets) ▲
- Paper bags (for puppets) ▲
- DVD or VHS recorder (for news reports) ● ■
- Scrapbooking materials ●

Special Notes on the Modifications of These Menus

- If needed, further modifications can be made to a 2-5-8 menu based on the needs of your students. The easiest modification is altering the point goal from 10; lowering or raising the goal on a menu by one (or two) points is appropriate if additional modification up or down is needed.

Special Notes on the Use of These Menus

- The circle and square menus give students the opportunity to create a news report. Although students enjoy producing their own videos, there often are difficulties obtaining the equipment and scheduling the use of a video recorder. This activity can be modified by allowing students to act out the news report (like a play) or, if students have the technology, allowing them to produce a webcam version of their product.
- These menus ask students to use recycled materials to create their trophies and models. This does not mean only plastic and paper; instead, students should focus on using materials in new ways. It works well if a box is started for "recycled" contributions at the beginning of the school year. That way, students always have access to these types of materials.

Time Frame

- 1–2 weeks—Students are given a menu as the story is started, and the teacher discusses all of the product options on the menu. As the different options are discussed, students will choose the activities they are most interested in completing so they meet their goal of 10 points. As the reading progresses through the week(s), the teacher and students refer back to the menu options associated with the content being taught.
- 1–2 days—The teacher chooses an activity or product from the menus to use with the entire class.

Suggested Forms

- All-purpose rubric
- Student presentation rubric
- Proposal form for point-based projects

The Lighthouse Family: The Storm

Directions: Choose at least two activities from the options below. The activities must total 10 points. Place a checkmark next to each box to show which activities you will complete. All activities must be completed by: _____.

2 Points

❑ Make a windowpane for six of the nautical words found in this story.

❑ Create a poster that shows what a lighthouse does to protect ships.

5 Points

❑ Design a special trophy for Seabold's brave actions with the mice.

❑ Pandora wants to give Seabold a friendship collage. Use words and pictures to create her collage.

❑ Complete a story map for *The Lighthouse Family: The Storm*.

❑ Free choice: Submit a proposal form for a product of your choice.

8 Points

❑ Make a set of puppets to retell the adventures of Pandora and Seabold.

❑ A local news reporter has heard about how Pandora has saved multiple lives this year. Record a news report about her job and how she has saved four lives.

The Lighthouse Family: The Storm

Directions: Choose at least two activities from the options below. The activities must total 10 points. Place a checkmark next to each box to show which activities you will complete. All activities must be completed by: _____.

2 Points

❏ Make a picture dictionary for all of the nautical words found in this story.

❏ Create a model of the lighthouse where Pandora works. Label all of the important parts.

5 Points

❏ Design a trophy for Seabold's brave actions. Include a paragraph explaining why he deserves the trophy.

❏ Create a scrapbook that Pandora could make to remember all of her adventures from the time she was a kitten until she meets the mice children.

❏ Make a folded quiz book for *The Lighthouse Family: The Storm*.

❏ Free choice: Submit a proposal form for a product of your choice.

8 Points

❏ Write a children's book about Seabold's life and adventures before he came to live with Pandora.

❏ A local news reporter has heard about how Pandora has saved multiple lives this year. Record a news report about her job and how she has saved four lives.

The Lighthouse Family: The Storm

Directions: Choose at least two activities from the options below. The activities must total 10 points. Place a checkmark next to each box to show which activities you will complete. All activities must be completed by: _____.

2 Points

❑ Make a picture dictionary for all of the nautical words found in this story.

❑ Create a lighthouse collage with words and pictures related to lighthouses. Name each picture.

5 Points

❑ A local news reporter has heard about how Pandora has saved multiple lives this year. Record a news report about her job and how she has saved four lives.

❑ Design a trophy for Seabold's brave actions. Include a paragraph explaining why he deserves the trophy.

❑ Make your own book cover for *The Lighthouse Family: The Storm*.

❑ Free choice: Submit a proposal form for a product of your choice.

8 Points

❑ Choose either the three small mice or Seabold, and write a children's book about their life and adventures before they came to live with Pandora.

❑ Keep a diary for Pandora that begins a few days before Seabold arrives and ends a few days after the story ends.

Charlotte's Web

Three-Topic List Menu

Fern saves a runt piglet from being slaughtered by her father. The piglet, Wilbur, is sold to another farm where he makes friends with the other animals and a very special spider, Charlotte. When Wilbur discovers that his life is again in danger, Charlotte spins a plan to keep Wilbur safe.

Reading Objectives Covered Through These Menus and These Activities

- Students will represent textual evidence and use it to prove conclusions.
- Students will make and explain inferences made from the story.
- Students will make predictions based on what is read.
- Students will show comprehension by retelling or acting out events in a story.
- Students will show comprehension by summarizing a story.
- Students will represent textual evidence by using story maps.
- Students will analyze characters, their relationships, and their importance in the story.

Writing Objectives Covered Through These Menus and These Activities

- Students will write to express their feelings, reflect, inform, explain, describe, entertain, or narrate.
- Students will write to influence or persuade.

Materials Needed by Students for Completion

- *Charlotte's Web* by E. B. White
- Poster board or large white paper
- Magazines (for collages)
- Story map ▲
- Recycled materials (for dioramas ▲ ●, trophies, models)
- Microsoft PowerPoint or other slideshow software ■
- DVD or VHS recorder (for commercials, news reports ● ■)
- Coat hangers (for mobiles) ▲ ●
- String (for mobiles) ▲ ●
- Blank index cards (for mobiles) ▲ ●

Special Note on the Modifications of These Menus

- Because a list menu is a point-based menu, it is easy to provide additional modifications by simply changing the point goal for those students who need it. The bottom of each menu has a short contract that can be used to record any changes in point goals.

Special Notes on the Use of These Menus

- These menus give students the opportunity to create commercials and news reports. Although students enjoy producing their own videos, there often are difficulties obtaining the equipment and scheduling the use of a video recorder. These activities can be modified by allowing students to act out the video (like a play) or, if students have the technology, allowing them to produce a webcam version of their product.
- These menus ask students to use recycled materials to create their dioramas, trophies, and models. This does not mean only plastic and paper; instead, students should focus on using materials in new ways. It works well if a box is started for "recycled" contributions at the beginning of the school year. That way, students always have access to these types of materials.

Time Frame

- 1–2 weeks—Students are given a menu as the story or novel unit is started, and the guidelines and point expectations are discussed. Students usually will need to earn 100 points for 100%, although there is an opportunity for extra credit if the teacher would like to use another target number. The students place check marks in the boxes next to the activities they are most interested in completing. As reading continues, additional explanation of the new activities can be provided. Once students have access to the entire menu, teachers will need to set aside a few moments to sign the agreement at the bottom of the page with each student. As activities are completed by students, they will be submitted to the teacher for grading.
- 1–2 days—The teacher chooses an activity or product from an objective to use with the entire class during that lesson time.

Suggested Forms

- All-purpose rubric
- Student presentation rubric
- Proposal form for point-based products

Name: _____

Charlotte's Web

Guidelines:

1. You may complete as many of the activities listed as you can within the time period.
2. You may choose any combination of activities, but **must** complete at least one activity from each topic area.
3. Your goal is 100 points. You may earn up to _____ points extra credit.
4. You may be as creative as you like within the guidelines listed below.
5. You must share your plan with your teacher by _____.
6. Activities may be turned in at any time during the working time period. They will be graded and recorded on this sheet as you continue to work, so keep it safe!

Topic	Plan to Do	Activity to Complete	Point Value	Date Completed	Points Earned
The Arable Farm		Make a collage of words and pictures to describe Fern.	15		
		Dramatically read the part of the story where Fern tries to convince her father to save the piglet.	20		
		Complete a story map for *Charlotte's Web*.	20		
		Build a diorama that shows Fern caring for Wilbur.	25		
		Design a brochure that Fern could have written sharing her ideas on how to properly care for a piglet.	30		
The Zuckerman Farm		Create a three facts and a fib about spiders.	15		
		Make a picture dictionary for at least five other words that Templeton could have found in newspaper clippings and brought to Charlotte.	15		
		Create a map that shows where all of the animals are located in the Zuckerman's barn.	20		
		Perform an interview with Lurvy about what he saw in the barn.	25		
		Create a commercial that Mr. Zuckerman could have used to bring people to his farm to see his marvelous pig.	30		
The Fair and Beyond		Research at least five different types of spiders. Make a flipbook to show three facts about each type of spider.	15		
		Charlotte and Wilbur have a special friendship. Create a mobile that shows at least three examples of the ways they support each other.	20		
		Create a trophy for the award that Wilbur won at the fair.	25		
		Pretend that you are Charlotte. Write a letter to Wilbur about your time with him.	30		
		Select a song that shows how you feel about the ending of *Charlotte's Web*. Play the song and tell how it shows the ending of the story.	30		
Any		**Free choice**: Submit your free choice proposal form for a product of your choice.			
		Total number of points you are planning to earn.		**Total points earned:**	

I am planning to complete _____ activities that could earn up to a total of _____ points.

Teacher's initials _____ Student's signature _____

Name: _____

Charlotte's Web

Guidelines:

1. You may complete as many of the activities listed as you can within the time period.
2. You may choose any combination of activities, but **must** complete at least one activity from each topic area.
3. Your goal is 100 points. You may earn up to _____ points extra credit.
4. You may be as creative as you like within the guidelines listed below.
5. You must share your plan with your teacher by _____.
6. Activities may be turned in at any time during the working time period. They will be graded and recorded on this sheet as you continue to work, so keep it safe!

Topic	Plan to Do	Activity to Complete	Point Value	Date Completed	Points Earned
The Arable Farm		Make a collage of words and pictures to describe Fern.	15		
		Dramatically read the part of the story where Fern tries to convince her father to save the piglet.	20		
		Build a diorama that shows Fern caring for Wilbur.	20		
		Create an advertisement that Mr. Arable could have used when he was ready to sell Wilbur to another farm.	25		
		Design a brochure that Fern could have written sharing her ideas on how to properly care for a piglet.	30		
The Zuckerman Farm		Create a three facts and a fib about rats.	15		
		Make a picture dictionary for at least eight other words that Templeton could have found in newspaper clippings and brought to Charlotte.	15		
		Create a map that shows where all of the animals are located in the Zuckerman's barn.	20		
		Create a commercial that Mr. Zuckerman could have used to bring people to his farm to see his marvelous pig.	25		
		Perform a news report about the "Some Pig" spider web. Be sure to interview Lurvy in your report.	30		
The Fair and Beyond		Research at least eight different types of spiders. Make a flipbook to show four facts about each type of spider.	15		
		Charlotte and Wilbur have a special friendship. Create a mobile that shows examples of all of the ways they support each other.	20		
		Create a trophy for the award that Wilbur won at the fair.	25		
		Pretend that you are Charlotte. Write a letter for Wilbur to read to your children when they arrive.	30		
		Write and perform a song about the ending of *Charlotte's Web*.	30		
Any		**Free choice**: Submit your free choice proposal form for a product of your choice.			
		Total number of points you are planning to earn.		**Total points earned:**	

I am planning to complete _____ activities that could earn up to a total of _____ points.

Teacher's initials _____ Student's signature _____

Name: _____   ■

Charlotte's Web

Guidelines:

1. You may complete as many of the activities listed as you can within the time period.
2. You may choose any combination of activities, but **must** complete at least one activity from each topic area.
3. Your goal is 100 points. You may earn up to _____ points extra credit.
4. You may be as creative as you like within the guidelines listed below.
5. You must share your plan with your teacher by _____.
6. Activities may be turned in at any time during the working time period. They will be graded and recorded on this sheet as you continue to work, so keep it safe!

Topic	Plan to Do	Activity to Complete	Point Value	Date Completed	Points Earned
The Arable Farm		Make a collage of words to describe Fern.	10		
		Dramatically read the part of the story where Fern tries to convince her father to save the piglet.	15		
		Make a greeting card that Fern could have given her father when he decided to let her to care for Wilbur.	20		
		Create an advertisement Mr. Arable could have used when he was ready to sell Wilbur.	25		
		Design a brochure that Fern could have written sharing her ideas on how to properly care for a piglet.	25		
The Zuckerman Farm		Create two different three facts and a fib, one about spiders and one about rats.	10		
		Make a picture dictionary for at least 10 other words that Templeton could have found in newspaper clippings and brought to Charlotte.	15		
		Create a model that shows the Zuckerman farm. Be sure and include where all of the animals are in the barn.	20		
		Create a commercial that Mr. Zuckerman could have used to bring people to his farm to see his marvelous pig.	25		
		Write a newspaper article about the "Some Pig" spider web. Be sure to interview Lurvy in your report.	25		
The Fair and Beyond		What kind of a spider do you think Charlotte is? Research this type of spider and its life span. Create a PowerPoint presentation to share your findings.	15		
		Consider all of the words that Charlotte used to describe Wilbur. Which word described him best? Make a poster with Wilbur and the word you picked, as well as a paragraph explaining why that word best describes Wilbur.	20		
		Create a trophy for the award that Wilbur won at the fair.	20		
		Pretend you are Charlotte and keep a diary from the time that you decide to go to the fair until the time Wilbur leaves.	25		
		Choose one quote from the entire book that you think is the most important. Make that quote part of a song and perform it for your classmates.	30		
Any		**Free choice**: Submit your free choice proposal form for a product of your choice.			
		Total number of points you are planning to earn.		**Total points earned:**	

I am planning to complete _____ activities that could earn up to a total of _____ points.

Teacher's initials _____ Student's signature _____

Sarah, Plain and Tall

2-5-8 Menu

A few years after Anna's mother dies after giving birth to Anna's brother Caleb, Anna's father decides to advertise for a bride to join them on the prairie. Their ad is answered by a young woman from Maine named Sarah. Sarah offers to come and visit the family to see if they can get along, but will she stay?

Reading Objectives Covered Through These Menus and These Activities

- Students will interpret figurative language and multiple meaning words.
- Students will make and explain inferences made from the story.
- Students will make predictions based on what is read.
- Students will show comprehension by retelling or acting out events in a story.
- Students will show comprehension by summarizing a story.
- Students will represent textual evidence by using story maps.

Writing Objectives Covered Through These Menus and These Activities

- Students will write to express their feelings, reflect, inform, explain, describe, or narrate.

Materials Needed by Students for Completion

- *Sarah, Plain and Tall* by Patricia MacLachlan
- Poster board or large white paper
- Blank index cards (for concentration cards)
- Recycled materials (for dioramas) ▲
- Story map
- Scrapbooking materials

Special Notes on the Modifications of These Menus

- If needed, further modifications can be made to a 2-5-8 menu based on the needs of your students. The easiest modification is altering the point goal from 10; lowering or raising the goal on a menu by one (or two) points is appropriate if additional modification up or down is needed.

Special Notes on the Use of These Menus

- The triangle ▲ menu asks students to use recycled materials to create their dioramas. This does not mean only plastic and paper; instead, students should focus on using materials in new ways. It works well if a box is started for "recycled" contributions at the beginning of the school year. That way, students always have access to these types of materials.

Time Frame

- 1–2 weeks—Students are given a menu as the story is started, and the teacher discusses all of the product options on the menu. As the different options are discussed, students will choose the activities they are most interested in completing so they meet their goal of 10 points. As the reading progresses through the week(s), the teacher and students refer back to the menu options associated with the content being taught.
- 1–2 days—The teacher chooses an activity or product from the menus to use with the entire class.

Suggested Forms

- All-purpose rubric
- Student presentation rubric
- Proposal form for point-based projects

Sarah, Plain and Tall

Directions: Choose at least two activities from the options below. The activities must total 10 points. Place a checkmark next to each box to show which activities you will complete. All activities must be completed by: _____.

2 Points

❑ Create a set of concentration cards for at least five vocabulary words from *Sarah, Plain and Tall.*

❑ Make an acrostic with the name of one of the characters. Place a word or phrase by each letter of his or her name telling something about him or her.

5 Points

❑ Complete a story map for *Sarah, Plain and Tall.*

❑ Sarah worked on the drawing of what she remembers about Maine. Create a drawing that would remind you of where you live.

❑ Create a greeting card that Caleb and Anna can give to Sarah when she arrives from Maine.

❑ Build a diorama that shows where the family lived.

8 Points

❑ Think about what might happen next for Anna's family. Tell a story about their life that starts at the point *Sarah, Plain and Tall* ended.

❑ Create a scrapbook that shares all of the details for the wedding of Jacob and Sarah.

Sarah, Plain and Tall

Directions: Choose at least two activities from the options below. The activities must total 10 points. Place a checkmark next to each box to show which activities you will complete. All activities must be completed by: _____.

2 Points

❏ Create a set of concentration cards for at least eight vocabulary words from *Sarah, Plain and Tall*.

❏ Complete a story map for *Sarah, Plain and Tall*.

5 Points

❏ Sarah worked on the drawing of what she remembers about Maine. Create a drawing that would remind you of where you live.

❏ Make a Venn diagram to compare and contrast Maine with the prairie. Think of as many things as you can!

❏ Create a greeting card that Caleb and Anna can give to Sarah when she arrives from Maine.

❏ Free choice: Submit a proposal form for a product of your choice.

8 Points

❏ Create a wedding scrapbook that shares all of the details for the wedding of Jacob and Sarah.

❏ Think about what might happen next for Anna's family. Write another chapter that starts at the point *Sarah, Plain and Tall* ended.

Sarah, Plain and Tall

Directions: Choose at least two activities from the options below. The activities must total 10 points. Place a checkmark next to each box to show which activities you will complete. All activities must be completed by: _____.

2 Points

❏ Create a set of concentration cards for at least 10 vocabulary words from *Sarah, Plain and Tall*.

❏ Complete a story map for *Sarah, Plain and Tall*.

5 Points

❏ Jacob placed an advertisement for a wife and mother. Design your own advertisement for someone or something you would like to add to your life.

❏ Sarah worked on the drawing of what she remembers about Maine. Create a drawing that would remind you of the state where you live.

❏ Make a Venn diagram to compare and contrast Maine with the prairie. Include at least two quotes to support your observations.

❏ Free choice: Submit a proposal form for a product of your choice.

8 Points

❏ Considering the time period and what is historically possible, create a wedding scrapbook for the wedding of Jacob and Sarah.

❏ Think about what might happen next for Anna's family. Write another chapter that starts at the point *Sarah, Plain and Tall* ended.

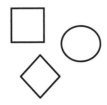

The One-Eyed Giant

Three Shape Menu ▲
and Tic-Tac-Toe Menu ● ■

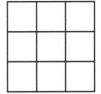

Odysseus is summoned to fight in a war against the Trojans. The Greeks find themselves at a disadvantage and are assisted by the goddess Athena. After executing her idea and winning the war, Odysseus and his men find that their journey home to Ithaca is not going to be an easy one. Storms, winds, and one-eyed giants will make the journey almost impossible.

Reading Objectives Covered Through These Menus and These Activities

- Students will make and explain inferences made from the story.
- Students will make predictions based on what is read.
- Students will show comprehension by retelling or acting out events in a story.
- Students will show comprehension by summarizing a story.
- Students will analyze characters, their relationships, and their importance in the story.

Writing Objectives Covered Through These Menus and These Activities

- Students will support their responses with textual evidence.
- Students will write to express their feelings, reflect, inform, explain, or describe.
- Students will write to influence or persuade. ■

Materials Needed by Students for Completion

- *The One-Eyed Giant* by Mary Pope Osborne
- Poster board or large white paper
- Blank index cards (for trading cards ▲)
- Recycled materials (for masks ▲, models ● ■, and puppets ▲)
- Socks (for puppets) ▲
- Paper bags (for puppets) ▲
- Microsoft PowerPoint or other slideshow software ● ■
- Scrapbooking materials ●
- DVD or VHS recorder (for news reports) ● ■
- Materials for bulletin board display ■

Special Notes on the Modifications of These Menus

- This topic has two different menu formats: the Three Shape menu (▲) and Tic-Tac-Toe (● ■) menu. The Three Shape menu is specifically selected for the triangle option, as it easily allows the menu to be broken into manageable bits; the three shapes visually separate the page, making it less daunting for special needs students. The space between the three shapes makes it easy for the teacher to cut the menu as needed based on the comfort level of the students. If it is the first time choice is being introduced, then the children may receive only the strip of the top row (or square) options. Then, when they have finished one of those options, they can receive a strip of circles and finally, the enrichment-level diamond activities. After students have grown more accustomed to making choices, the menu might be cut just once after the circles, so students can select a square and a circle and submit them to the teacher. Then, they can choose from the diamond strip they receive. The ultimate goal would be for students to have all nine options at once and not be overwhelmed.

Special Notes on the Use of These Menus

- The circle and square menus ● ■ give students the opportunity to create a news report. Although students enjoy producing their own videos, there often are difficulties obtaining the equipment and scheduling the use of a video recorder. This activity can be modified by allowing students to act out the news report (like a play) or, if students have the technology, allowing them to produce a webcam version of their product.
- These menus ask students to use recycled materials to create their masks, models, and puppets. This does not mean only plastic and paper; instead, students should focus on using materials in new ways. It works well if a box is started for "recycled" contributions at the beginning of the school year. That way, students always have access to these types of materials.
- The square menu ■ allows students to create a bulletin board display. Some classrooms may only have one bulletin board, so the teacher can divide the board into sections, or additional classroom wall or hall space can be sectioned off for the creation of these displays. Students can plan their display based on the amount of space they are assigned.

Time Frame

- 1–3 weeks—Students are given a menu as the story or novel is started. As reading progresses and the teacher presents lessons throughout the week, he or she should refer back to the menu options associated with that content. The teacher will go over all of the options for the story and have students indicate the activities they are most interested in completing. When using the Tic-Tac-Toe format, students should complete a column or a row. If they are using the Three Shape format, students will be completing an activity for each of the three shapes. When students complete these patterns, they have completed one activity from each content area, learning style, or level of Bloom's revised taxonomy, depending on the design of the menu.

- 1 week–At the start of the unit, the teacher chooses the three activities he or she feels are most valuable for students. Stations can be set up in the classroom. These three activities are available for student choice throughout the week as regular instruction takes place.
- 1–2 days—The teacher chooses an activity from the menus to use with the entire class.

Suggested Forms

- All-purpose rubric
- Student presentation rubric
- Free-choice proposal form

The One-Eyed Giant

Directions: Circle one choice from each group of shapes. Color in the shape after you have finished it. All products are due by : _____.

Create a set of trading cards for five of the important characters in this story.

Draw a timeline to show all of the adventures Odysseus has had so far. Start your timeline at his home.

Make an acrostic for the word *Cyclops*. Use a word or phrase for each letter to describe this creature.

Design a Cyclops mask. Write a paragraph about your mask, describing the creature.

The Trojan horse has become a famous strategy. Make a drawing of the Trojan horse that shows the inside of the horse.

Free choice: Submit a proposal form for a product of your choice.

Using a puppet you have made, tell what happened at the battle of Troy.

Pretend you are Odysseus and tell your classmates about your favorite adventure so far.

Perform a play that retells the story of Odysseus's escape from the Cyclops's island.

The One-Eyed Giant

Directions: Check the boxes you plan to complete. They should form a tic-tac-toe across or down. All products are due by: _____.

☐ **The Odyssey Begins**	☐ **Tell the Story of the Hero**	☐ **The Trojan Horse**
Create a PowerPoint presentation to share the events that led up Odysseus's return to see Aeolus.	Perform a play that retells the story of Odysseus's escape from Polyphemus's viewpoint.	The Trojan horse has become a famous strategy. Build a model of the Trojan horse that shows how it was used in this battle.
☐ **The Cyclops**	☐ **Free Choice: The Trojan Horse** (Fill out your proposal form before beginning the free choice!)	☐ **Tell the Story of the Hero**
Research Polyphemus. Create a scrapbook about his family, his name, and what he likes to do each day.		Perform a speech that Odysseus could have given to Aeolus to try and change his mind the second time he spoke to him.
☐ **Tell the Story of the Hero**	☐ **The Flower of Forgetfulness**	☐ **The Cyclops' Island**
Create a news report that covers the war in Troy. Discuss the reasons for war, as well as what brings it to an end.	Three of Odysseus's men ate the flower of "forgetfulness." Write and perform a song about this flower and what it does to people who eat it.	Based on the information in the story, draw a map of Polyphemus's island. Be sure to label all of the locations, including Odysseus's ships.

Name: _____

The One-Eyed Giant

Directions: Check the boxes you plan to complete. They should form a tic-tac-toe across or down. All products are due by: _____.

☐ **The Next Chapter** Think about what Polyphemus yelled to Odysseus and how Aeolus responded to Odysseus when he returned. Write a story of Odysseus's return to Ithaca.	☐ **Tell the Story of the Hero** Before stories were recorded, people would sing songs about others who had completed marvelous feats. Create a song about Odysseus and his experience with Polyphemus.	☐ **The Trojan Horse** The Trojan horse has become a famous strategy. Research another event in history that was similar to the Trojan horse. Create a bulletin board display to share your research with your classmates.
☐ **The Cyclops** The story gives us information on the Cyclops species. Create a poster to share where they come from, their habitat, and other important facts.	☐ **Free Choice:** **The Trojan Horse** (Fill out your proposal form before beginning the free choice!)	☐ **Tell the Story of the Hero** If there had been television in Odysseus's time, he surely would have made the news! Create a news report covering his negotiations with Aeolus.
☐ **Tell the Story of the Hero** Perform a play that retells the story of the Trojan Horse from Athena's perceptive.	☐ **The Flower of Forgetfulness** Three of Odysseus's men ate the flower of "forgetfulness." Research this flower and create a PowerPoint presentation to share your findings with your classmates.	☐ **The Cyclops' Cave** Based on the information in the story, create a model of Polyphemus's cave. It should be able to demonstrate how Odysseus and his men escaped.

My Father's Dragon

List Menu

When Elmer Elevator, the father of our narrator, was just a boy he took in an old alley cat. His family did not like the cat and he was punished for feeding it. Elmer snuck out to be with the cat and began commenting that he wished he could fly. The cat suggests a way he may be able to fly; however, it will involve running away and saving a dragon. They embark on a wild adventure that neither would ever forget.

Reading Objectives Covered Through These Menus and These Activities

- Students will represent textual evidence and use it to prove conclusions.
- Students will make and explain inferences made from the story.
- Students will make predictions based on what is read.
- Students will show comprehension by retelling or acting out events in a story.
- Students will show comprehension by summarizing a story.
- Students will represent textual evidence by using story maps.
- Students will recognize and analyze story plot and problem resolution.

Writing Objectives Covered Through These Menus and These Activities

- Students will write to express their feelings, reflect, inform, explain, describe, entertain, or narrate.
- Students will support their responses with textual evidence.

Materials Needed by Students for Completion

- *My Father's Dragon* by Ruth Stiles Gannett
- Poster board or large white paper
- Blank index cards (for trading cards, concentration cards ▲)
- Socks (for puppets)
- Paper bags (for puppets)
- Recycled materials (for puppets)
- DVD or VHS recorder (for commercials)
- Microsoft PowerPoint or other slideshow software ■
- Story map ▲ ●
- Large lined index cards (for instruction cards) ●
- Magazines (for collages) ▲
- Materials for board games (folders, colored cards, etc.) ▲

Special Notes on the Modifications of These Menus

- Because a list menu is a point-based menu, it is easy to provide additional modifications by simply changing the point goal for those students who need it. The bottom of the menu has a short contract that can be used to record any changes. The two-page format of the triangle and circle menu also allow for additional modification by mixing and matching the pages. The front of each of these two-page menus has the lower and middle-level activities, while the second page has the higher level activities and contract. Additional modifications can be made by using the first page from the circle menu with the second page from the triangle menu. This will allow students a little more flexibility when approaching the higher level activities.

Special Notes on the Use of These Menus

- These menus give students the opportunity to create a commercial. Although students enjoy producing their own videos, there often are difficulties obtaining the equipment and scheduling the use of a video recorder. This activity can be modified by allowing students to act out the product (like a play) or, if students have the technology, allowing them to produce a webcam version of their product.
- These menus ask students to use recycled materials to create their puppets. This does not mean only plastic and paper; instead, students should focus on using materials in new ways. It works well if a box is started for "recycled" contributions at the beginning of the school year. That way, students always have access to these types of materials.

Time Frame

- 1–2 weeks—Students are given a menu as the reading of the story is started, and the guidelines and point expectations are discussed. Students usually will need to earn 100 points for 100%, although there is an opportunity for extra credit if the teacher would like to use another target number. Because this menu covers the story in depth, the teacher will go over all of the options for the work being covered and have students place check marks in the boxes next to the activities they are most interested in completing. Teachers will need to set aside a few moments to sign the agreement at the bottom of the page with each student. As reading continues, activities are completed by students and submitted to the teacher for grading.
- 1–2 days—The teacher chooses an activity or product from an objective to use with the entire class during that lesson time.

Suggested Forms

- All-purpose rubric
- Student presentation rubric
- Proposal form for point-based products

Name: _____ ▲

My Father's Dragon: Side 1

Guidelines:

1. You may complete as many of the activities listed within the time period.
2. You may choose any combination of activities.
3. Your goal is 100 points. You may earn up to _____ points extra credit.
4. You may be as creative as you like within the guidelines listed below.
5. You must show your plan to your teacher by _____.
6. Activities may be turned in at any time during the working time period. They will be graded and recorded on this sheet as you continue to work, so keep it safe!

Plan to Do	Activity to Complete (Side 1: 15–25 points)	Point Value	Date Completed	Points Earned
	Make a set of concentration cards to match the animal with the item Elmer brought for it.	15		
	Create a drawing that could be put on the cover of *My Father's Dragon*.	15		
	Submit a story map for *My Father's Dragon*.	15		
	Create a collage of words and drawings to share the plot of this story.	15		
	Make trading cards for three of the animals that Elmer meets on Wild Island.	20		
	Write an acrostic for *Elmer*. Include words or phrases about his character traits for each letter.	20		
	Build a three-dimensional timeline for the story that shares all of the major events that took place.	25		
	Draw an advertisement to sell one of the products that Elmer gave to an animal on Wild Island.	25		
	Prepare a Venn diagram to compare one of the animals in the book with that same animal found in the wild.	25		
	Total number of points you are planning to earn from Side 1.		**Total points earned from Side 1:**	

My Father's Dragon: Side 2

Guidelines:

1. You may complete as many of the activities listed within the time period.
2. You may choose any combination of activities.
3. Your goal is 100 points. You may earn up to _____ points extra credit.
4. You may be as creative as you like within the guidelines listed below.
5. You must show your plan to your teacher by _____.
6. Activities may be turned in at any time during the working time period. They will be graded and recorded on this sheet as you continue to work, so keep it safe!

Plan to Do	Activity to Complete (Side 2: 30–40 points)	Point Value	Date Completed	Points Earned
	Compose the letter that Elmer could have left behind for his mother to explain why he ran away.	30		
	Design a dragon puppet and have it tell about its experiences on Wild Island.	30		
	Make a board game about Elmer Elevator's adventures during the time he ran away from home.	30		
	On a poster, create a map of Wild Island. Be sure to include the locations of all of the animals on the map.	35		
	Pretend you are one of the animals who wants people to stay away from Wild Island. Create a commercial that tells why people should not visit.	35		
	Write and perform a song about the mighty Elmer and how he became a hero.	35		
	With the help of your classmates, direct and perform a short skit about Elmer's rescue mission.	40		
	Free choice: Submit your free choice proposal form for a product of your choice.			
	Total number of points you are planning to earn from Side 1.	**Total points earned from Side 1:**		
	Total number of points you are planning to earn from Side 2.	**Total points earned from Side 2:**		
		Grand Total (/100)		

I am planning to complete _____ activities that could earn up to a total of _____ points.

Teacher's initials _____ Student's signature _____

Name: _____

My Father's Dragon: Side 1

Guidelines:

1. You may complete as many of the activities listed within the time period.
2. You may choose any combination of activities.
3. Your goal is 100 points. You may earn up to _____ points extra credit.
4. You may be as creative as you like within the guidelines listed below.
5. You must show your plan to your teacher by _____.
6. Activities may be turned in at any time during the working time period. They will be graded and recorded on this sheet as you continue to work, so keep it safe!

Plan to Do	Activity to Complete (Side 1: 10–20 points)	Point Value	Date Completed	Points Earned
	Make a windowpane to show the different items that the cat told Elmer to bring. Beside each item, tell why he needed to bring each item.	10		
	Submit a story map for *My Father's Dragon*.	10		
	Design a new book cover for *My Father's Dragon*.	15		
	Make a set of trading cards for all of the animals that Elmer meets on Wild Island.	15		
	Make an acrostic for *Elmer Elevator*. Include words or phrases about his character traits for each letter.	15		
	Build a three-dimensional timeline for the story that shares all of the major events that took place.	20		
	Draw an advertisement to sell one of the products that Elmer gave to an animal on Wild Island.	20		
	Prepare a Venn diagram to compare one of the animals in the book with that same animal found in the wild.	20		
	Write an instruction card to tell the steps needed in rescuing a dragon from Wild Island.	20		
	Total number of points you are planning to earn from Side 1.	**Total points earned from Side 1:**		

Name: _____ ●

My Father's Dragon: Side 2

Guidelines:

1. You may complete as many of the activities listed within the time period.
2. You may choose any combination of activities.
3. Your goal is 100 points. You may earn up to _____ points extra credit.
4. You may be as creative as you like within the guidelines listed below.
5. You must show your plan to your teacher by _____.
6. Activities may be turned in at any time during the working time period. They will be graded and recorded on this sheet as you continue to work, so keep it safe!

Plan to Do	Activity to Complete (Side 2: 25–35 points)	Point Value	Date Completed	Points Earned
	Compose the letter that Elmer could have left behind for his mother to explain why he ran away.	25		
	Design a dragon puppet and have it tell about its experiences on Wild Island.	25		
	On a poster, create a map of Tangerina and Wild Island. Be sure to include the locations of all of the animals on the map.	30		
	Pretend you are a travel agent who wants more people to visit Wild Island. Create a commercial that tells why tourists should travel to the island.	30		
	Write a newspaper article that describes Elmer Elevator's adventure during the time he ran away from home.	30		
	Write and perform a song about the mighty Elmer and how he became a hero.	30		
	Elmer gave an item to each animal on Wild Island to distract it. Write a children's book to tell the story of two of the animals and why they liked their gift.	35		
	Free choice: Submit your free choice proposal form for a product of your choice.			
	Total number of points you are planning to earn from Side 1.	**Total points earned from Side 1:**		
	Total number of points you are planning to earn from Side 2.	**Total points earned from Side 2:**		
		Grand Total (/100)		

I am planning to complete _____ activities that could earn up to a total of _____ points.

Teacher's initials _____ Student's signature _____

Name: _____ ■

My Father's Dragon

Guidelines:

1. You may complete as many of the activities listed within the time period.
2. You may choose any combination of activities.
3. Your goal is 100 points. You may earn up to _____ points extra credit.
4. You may be as creative as you like within the guidelines listed below.
5. You must show your plan to your teacher by _____.
6. Activities may be turned in at any time during the working time period. They will be graded and recorded on this sheet as you continue to work, so keep it safe!

Plan to Do	Activity to Complete	Point Value	Date Completed	Points Earned
	Make a windowpane to show the different items that the cat told Elmer to bring. Beside each item, tell why he needed to bring each item.	10		
	Design a new book cover for *My Father's Dragon*.	15		
	Design a three-dimensional timeline for the story that shares all of the major events that took place.	15		
	Make a set of trading cards for all of the animals that Elmer meets on Wild Island.	15		
	Make a T-chart of characteristics, places, and events to show what aspects of the story are based on fact and which are fiction.	15		
	Compose the letter that Elmer could have left behind for his mother to explain why he ran away.	20		
	Design a dragon puppet and have it tell about its experiences on Wild Island.	20		
	Draw an advertisement to sell one of the products that Elmer gave to an animal on Wild Island.	20		
	Prepare a Venn diagram to compare one of the animals in the book with that same animal found in the wild.	20		
	On a poster, create a map of Tangerina and Wild Island. Be sure to include the locations of all of the animals on the map.	25		
	Pretend you are a travel agent who wants more people to visit Tangerina. Create a commercial that tells why tourists should travel to the island.	25		
	Write a newspaper article that describes Elmer Elevator's adventure during the time he ran away from home.	25		
	Elmer gave an item to each animal on Wild Island to distract it. Write a children's book to tell the story of each animal and why it liked its gift.	30		
	Elmer used certain things from home to distract each of the animals. Were those the only items that could distract them? Design a PowerPoint presentation to share other items that could have distracted each of the animals. Include why you think each would be a good distraction.	30		
	Write and perform a song about the mighty Elmer and how he became a hero.	30		
	Free choice: Submit your free choice proposal form for a product of your choice.			
	Total number of points you are planning to earn.		**Total points earned:**	

I am planning to complete _____ activities that could earn up to a total of _____ points.

Teacher's initials _____ Student's signature _____

Mr. Popper's Penguins

List Menu

After Mr. Popper, a painter, expresses an interest in Admiral Drake's expedition to the South Pole and his encounters with penguins, Admiral Drake surprises him with a penguin of his very own. The adventures continue as the Poppers decide how to keep the penguin happy in their warm climate. After many adventures, the Poppers end up with a large family of penguins that help them completely change their lives.

Reading Objectives Covered Through These Menus and These Activities

- Students will make and explain inferences made from the story.
- Students will make predictions based on what is read.
- Students will show comprehension by retelling or acting out events in a story.
- Students will show comprehension by summarizing a story.
- Students will represent textual evidence by using story maps.
- Students will recognize and analyze story plot and problem resolution.

Writing Objectives Covered Through These Menus and These Activities

- Students will write to express their feelings, reflect, inform, explain, describe, or narrate.
- Students will support their responses with textual evidence.

Materials Needed by Students for Completion

- *Mr. Popper's Penguins* by Richard and Florence Atwater
- Poster board or large white paper
- Socks (for puppets)
- Paper bags (for puppets)
- Recycled materials (for dioramas, puppets)
- Coat hangers (for mobiles)
- String (for mobiles)
- Blank index cards (for mobiles, trading cards)
- Microsoft PowerPoint or other slideshow software ■
- Story map ▲
- DVD or VHS recorder (for commercials)
- Scrapbooking materials
- Magazines (for collages) ●
- World map ● ■

- Ruler (for comic strip) ▲
- Graph paper or Internet access (for crossword puzzles) ●

Special Notes on the Modifications of These Menus

- Because a list menu is a point-based menu, it is easy to provide additional modifications by simply changing the point goal for those students who need it. The bottom of the menu has a short contract that can be used to record any changes. The two-page format of the triangle and circle menu also allow for additional modification by mixing and matching the pages. The front of each of these two-page menus has the lower and middle level activities, while the second page has the higher level activities and contract. Additional modifications can be made by using the first page from the circle menu with the second page from the triangle menu. This will allow students a little more flexibility when approaching the higher level activities.

Special Notes on the Use of These Menus

- These menus give students the opportunity to create commercials and news reports. Although students enjoy producing their own videos, there often are difficulties obtaining the equipment and scheduling the use of a video recorder. This activity can be modified by allowing students to act out their products (like a play) or, if students have the technology, allowing them to produce a webcam version of their product.
- These menus ask students to use recycled materials to create their dioramas and puppets. This does not mean only plastic and paper; instead, students should focus on using materials in new ways. It works well if a box is started for "recycled" contributions at the beginning of the school year. That way, students always have access to these types of materials.

Time Frame

- 1–2 weeks—Students are given a menu as the reading of the story is started, and the guidelines and point expectations are discussed. Students usually will need to earn 100 points for 100%, although there is an opportunity for extra credit if the teacher would like to use another target number. Because this menu covers the story in depth, the teacher will go over all of the options for the work being covered and have students place check marks in the boxes next to the activities they are most interested in completing. Teachers will need to set aside a few moments to sign the agreement at the bottom of the page with each student. As reading continues, activities are completed by students and submitted to the teacher for grading.

- 1–2 days—The teacher chooses an activity or product from an objective to use with the entire class during that lesson time.

Suggested Forms

- All-purpose rubric
- Student presentation rubric
- Proposal form for point-based products

Mr. Popper's Penguins: Side 1

Guidelines:

1. You may complete as many of the activities listed within the time period.
2. You may choose any combination of activities.
3. Your goal is 100 points. You may earn up to _____ points extra credit.
4. You may be as creative as you like within the guidelines listed below.
5. You must show your plan to your teacher by _____.
6. Activities may be turned in at any time during the working time period. They will be graded and recorded on this sheet as you continue to work, so keep it safe!

Plan to Do	Activity to Complete (Side 1: 10–25 points)	Point Value	Date Completed	Points Earned
	Draw a window pane that shows a drawing of each penguin in the order that they come to live with Mr. Popper.	10		
	Complete a story map for *Mr. Popper's Penguins*.	15		
	Design a picture dictionary for at least eight vocabulary words found in the story.	15		
	Read about the types of penguins found at the South Pole and create a poster about these penguins.	15		
	Create a diorama to show the stage performance you liked best in the story.	20		
	Build a mobile with examples of facts and fiction about penguins found in the story.	20		
	Create a set of trading cards for five of the penguins in the story. Include information on their likes and dislikes.	20		
	Make a timeline that shows Admiral Drake's expedition through Antarctica.	25		
	Mr. Popper's penguins were selected to advertise Owens Oceanic Shrimp. Create an advertisement for another product that the penguins could advertise.	25		
	Total number of points you are planning to earn from Side 1.	**Total points earned from Side 1:**		

Mr. Popper's Penguins: Side 2

Guidelines:

1. You may complete as many of the activities listed within the time period.
2. You may choose any combination of activities.
3. Your goal is 100 points. You may earn up to _____ points extra credit.
4. You may be as creative as you like within the guidelines listed below.
5. You must show your plan to your teacher by _____.
6. Activities may be turned in at any time during the working time period. They will be graded and recorded on this sheet as you continue to work, so keep it safe!

Plan to Do	Activity to Complete (Side 2: 30–40 points)	Point Value	Date Completed	Points Earned
	At the end of the story, Mr. Popper has to make a decision. Write a letter to Mr. Popper telling him what you think he should do and why.	30		
	Draw a comic strip to show what happened when the penguins were on the bus.	30		
	Write and sing a song about Mr. Popper's crazy winter.	30		
	Research the famous names Mr. Popper chose for his male penguins and create a puppet for one of these people. Have your puppet share information about its accomplishments with your classmates.	35		
	What wild animal would you like to have as a pet? How would you need to change your home to accommodate it? Write a children's book about your "wild" pet and its life in your home.	35		
	Write a journal entry from Captain Cook's point of view that talks about his time with the Poppers.	35		
	What will happen next to Mr. Popper? Create a scrapbook to share what happened next after the story ended.	40		
	Free choice: Submit your free choice proposal form for a product of your choice.			
	Total number of points you are planning to earn from Side 1.	**Total points earned from Side 1:**		
	Total number of points you are planning to earn from Side 2.	**Total points earned from Side 2:**		
		Grand Total (/100)		

I am planning to complete _____ activities that could earn up to a total of _____ points.

Teacher's initials _____ Student's signature _____

Name: _____

Mr. Popper's Penguins: Side 1

Guidelines:

1. You may complete as many of the activities listed within the time period.
2. You may choose any combination of activities.
3. Your goal is 100 points. You may earn up to _____ points extra credit.
4. You may be as creative as you like within the guidelines listed below.
5. You must show your plan to your teacher by _____.
6. Activities may be turned in at any time during the working time period. They will be graded and recorded on this sheet as you continue to work, so keep it safe!

Plan to Do	Activity to Complete (Side 1: 10–20 points)	Point Value	Date Completed	Points Earned
	Design a picture dictionary for at least 10 vocabulary words found in the story. Include the sentence from the book that has the word.	10		
	Create a collage of words that could be used to describe one of the characters in *Mr. Popper's Penguins*.	10		
	Design a diorama to show the stage performance you liked best in the story.	15		
	Make a mobile with examples of things that are true about penguins and things that are made up in the story.	15		
	On a world map, locate where penguins live. Mark each area with the type of penguin found there.	15		
	Design a thank you card that Mr. Popper could send to Admiral Drake when his surprise arrived in the mail.	20		
	Mr. Popper's penguins were selected to advertise Owens Oceanic Shrimp. Develop an advertisement for another product that the penguins could advertise.	20		
	Research the types of penguins found at the South Pole and make a crossword puzzle with information about each of these types of penguins.	20		
	Create a set of trading cards for each of the penguins, including information on their likes and dislikes.	20		
	Total number of points you are planning to earn from Side 1.	**Total points earned from Side 1:**		

Name: _____   ●

Mr. Popper's Penguins: Side 2

Guidelines:

1. You may complete as many of the activities listed within the time period.
2. You may choose any combination of activities.
3. Your goal is 100 points. You may earn up to _____ points extra credit.
4. You may be as creative as you like within the guidelines listed below.
5. You must show your plan to your teacher by _____.
6. Activities may be turned in at any time during the working time period. They will be graded and recorded on this sheet as you continue to work, so keep it safe!

Plan to Do	Activity to Complete (Side 2: 25–35 points)	Point Value	Date Completed	Points Earned
	At the end of the story, Mr. Popper has to make a decision. Write a letter to Mr. Popper telling him what you think he should do and why.	25		
	Research the famous names Mr. Popper chose for his male penguins and make a puppet for one of these people. Have your puppet share information about his accomplishments.	30		
	What wild animal would you like to have as a pet? How would you need to change your home to accommodate it? Write a children's book about your "wild" pet and its life in your home.	30		
	Write and sing a song about Mr. Popper's crazy winter.	30		
	Research Admiral Drake's expedition through Antarctica. Come to class as Admiral Drake prepared to talk about your adventures.	35		
	What will happen next? Create a scrapbook to share the adventures after the story ended.	35		
	Free choice: Submit your free choice proposal form for a product of your choice.			
	Total number of points you are planning to earn from Side 1.	**Total points earned from Side 1:**		
	Total number of points you are planning to earn from Side 2.	**Total points earned from Side 2:**		
		Grand Total (/100)		

I am planning to complete _____ activities that could earn up to a total of _____ points.

Teacher's initials _____ Student's signature _____

Name: _____ ■

Mr. Popper's Penguins

Guidelines:

1. You may complete as many of the activities listed within the time period.
2. You may choose any combination of activities.
3. Your goal is 100 points. You may earn up to _____ points extra credit.
4. You may be as creative as you like within the guidelines listed below.
5. You must show your plan to your teacher by _____.
6. Activities may be turned in at any time during the working time period. They will be graded and recorded on this sheet as you continue to work, so keep it safe!

Plan to Do	Activity to Complete	Point Value	Date Completed	Points Earned
	Write a picture dictionary for at least 10 vocabulary words found in the story. Include the sentence from the book that has the word.	10		
	Design a diorama to show the stage performance you liked best in the story.	10		
	On a world map, locate where penguins live. Mark each area with the type of penguin found there.	10		
	Make a mobile with examples of facts and fiction about penguins found in the story. Include a quote for each example.	15		
	Are penguins only in cold regions? Research the different types of penguins found around the world and write a three facts and a fib about these penguins to share with your class.	20		
	In addition to entertaining people, animals can be trained for different purposes. Research other ways that animals are trained and prepare a PowerPoint presentation to share your findings.	20		
	Mr. Popper's penguins were selected to advertise Owens Oceanic Shrimp. Think of another product that the penguins could advertise. Develop a commercial for this new product.	20		
	Create a set of trading cards for each of the penguins, including information on their likes and dislikes. Include a quote from the story about each penguin.	20		
	Mr. Popper wrote a letter to Admiral Drake about his expedition. Choose someone who is doing something you find interesting and write him or her a letter telling what you think is most interesting about his or her work.	25		
	Research Admiral Drake's expedition through Antarctica. Come to class as Admiral Drake, prepared to talk about your adventures.	25		
	Research the famous names Mr. Popper chose for his male penguins and create a puppet for one of these people. Have your puppet share information about his accomplishments with your classmates.	25		
	At the end of the story, Mr. Popper has to make a decision. Write a newspaper editorial article about his decision and whether you agree or not.	30		
	Write a journal entry from Captain Cook's point of view that talks about his first day with the Poppers.	30		
	What will happen next to Mr. Popper? Design a scrapbook to share what happened next after the story ended.	30		
	After finishing the story and with your parents' permission, watch the movie *Mr. Popper's Penguins*. Would the authors be happy with the movie? Come to class as Richard or Florence Atwater and discuss your impressions of the movie compared to the story you wrote.	30		
	Free choice: Submit your free choice proposal form for a product of your choice.			
	Total number of points you are planning to earn.		**Total points earned:**	

I am planning to complete _____ activities that could earn up to a total of _____ points.

Teacher's initials _____ Student's signature _____

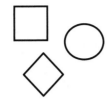

The Birchbark House

Three Shape Menu ▲ and Tic-Tac-Toe Menu ● ■

Omakayas, a young Ojibwa girl, has a lot of responsibilities in her family, especially as they prepare for winter. She helps tan hides, serves as a human scarecrow, and tends to her family when they get sick during the winter. When smallpox finds its way to their village, Omakayas is faced with a decision and then, the consequences of her choice.

Reading Objectives Covered Through These Menus and These Activities

- Students will make and explain inferences made from the story.
- Students will make predictions based on what is read.
- Students will show comprehension by retelling or acting out events in a story.
- Students will show comprehension by summarizing a story.
- Students will analyze characters, their relationships, and their importance in the story.
- Students will recognize and analyze story plot and problem resolution.

Writing Objectives Covered Through These Menus and These Activities

- Students will write to express their feelings, reflect, inform, explain, describe, entertain, or narrate.

Materials Needed by Students for Completion

- *The Birchbark House* by Louise Erdrich
- Poster board or large white paper
- Map of the United States
- Microsoft PowerPoint or other slideshow software ■
- Large lined index cards (for instruction cards) ■
- DVD or VHS recorder (for videos)
- Coat hangers (for mobiles) ■
- String (for mobiles) ■
- Blank index cards (for mobiles) ■
- Recycled materials (for models ●　■, dioramas ▲)

Special Notes on the Modifications of These Menus

- This topic has two different menu formats: the Three Shape menu (▲) and Tic-Tac-Toe (● ■) menu. The Three Shape menu is specifically selected for the triangle option, as it easily allows the menu to be broken into manageable bits; the three shapes visually separate the page, making it less daunting for special needs students. The space between the three shapes makes it easy for the teacher to cut the menu as needed based on the comfort level of the students. If it is the first time choice is being introduced, then the children may receive only the strip of the top row or square options. Then, when they have finished one of those options, they can receive a strip of circles and finally, the enrichment-level diamond activities. After students have grown more accustomed to making choices, the menu might be cut just once after the circles, so students can select a square and a circle and submit them to the teacher. Then, they can choose from the diamond strip they receive. The ultimate goal would be for students to have all nine options at once and not be overwhelmed.

Special Notes on the Use of These Menus

- These menus give students the opportunity to create a video. Although students enjoy producing their own videos, there often are difficulties obtaining the equipment and scheduling the use of a video recorder. This activity can be modified by allowing students to act out their video (like a play) or, if students have the technology, allowing them to produce a webcam version of their product.
- This menu asks students to use recycled materials to create their models and dioramas. This does not mean only plastic and paper; instead, students should focus on using materials in new ways. It works well if a box is started for "recycled" contributions at the beginning of the school year. That way, students always have access to these types of materials.

Time Frame

- 1–3 weeks—Students are given a menu as the story or novel is started. As reading progresses and the teacher presents lessons throughout the week, he or she should refer back to the menu options associated with that content. The teacher will go over all of the options for the story and have students indicate the activities they are most interested in completing. When using the Tic-Tac-Toe format, students should complete a column or a row. If they are using the Three Shape format, students will be completing an activity for each of the three shapes. When students complete these patterns, they have completed one activity from each content area, learning style, or level of Bloom's revised taxonomy, depending on the design of the menu.

- 1 week–At the start of the unit, the teacher chooses the three activities he or she feels are most valuable for students. Stations can be set up in the classroom. These three activities are available for student choice throughout the week as regular instruction takes place.
- 1–2 days—The teacher chooses an activity from the menus to use with the entire class.

Suggested Forms

- All-purpose rubric
- Student presentation rubric
- Free-choice proposal form

The Birchbark House

Directions: Circle one choice from each group of shapes. Color in the shape after you have finished it. All products are due by : _____.

Using a map of the United States, show where tribal nations lived across the United States during the time period when this story took place. Be sure and include where Omakayas lived.

Make a drawing that could have been used to provide information about smallpox to the Indians.

Make a poster to show reasons why Native Americans might want to learn to read and speak English.

Use a Venn diagram to compare Omakayas's life with your life when you were her age.

Make a drawing or family portrait that includes all of the members of Omakayas's family (including Old Tallow).

Create a diorama of the town that Omakayas and her family visit after the first snow. Be sure and label all of the buildings and what happens in each one.

Three important oral stories were told by characters in this novel. Create a video that shares the most important story.

Pretend you are Andeg. Write three journal entries, one for how you meet Omakayas, one when you hear the other crows, and one when you land on Pinch's shoulder.

Bears play an important role in this novel. Perform a song about what happens each time that Omakayas meets a bear in the novel.

The Birchbark House

Directions: Check the boxes you plan to complete. They should form a tic-tac-toe across or down. All products are due by: _____.

☐ **Tribal Nation Map** Using a map of the United States, show where tribal nations lived across the United States during the time period when this story took place. Be sure and include where Omakayas lived.	☐ **Your Life and Omakayas's Life** Use a Venn diagram to compare Omakayas's life with your life when you were her age.	☐ **Building a Birchbark House** Build a small model of a birchbark house. Include a list of the materials you used to build it.
☐ **Telling Stories** Three important oral stories were told by characters in this novel. Create a video that shares two of these stories. Include who told each story and what happened in each story.	☐ **Free Choice: The Birchbark House** (Fill out your proposal form before beginning the free choice!)	☐ **A Family Portrait** Make a drawing or family portrait that includes all of the members of Omakayas's family (including Old Tallow).
☐ **Andeg's Journal** Pretend you are Andeg. Write four journal entries that share his thoughts on his time with Omakayas. Be sure and include your thoughts at the end of the novel.	☐ **Omakayas and the Bears** Bears play an important role in this novel. Write and perform a song about the importance of bears in Omakayas's life. It should be a traditional song that might have been sung in the dance lodge.	☐ **Investigating Smallpox** Design a poster that could have been used at the time to provide information on smallpox. Include how to identify the disease, how to prevent it, and its possible treatments.

The Birchbark House

Directions: Check the boxes you plan to complete. They should form a tic-tac-toe across or down. All products are due by: _____.

☐ **Tribal Nation Map** Using a map of the United States, indicate where tribal nations lived across the United States. Be sure to include where Omakayas lives. On the same map, indicate where tribal nations live now in the United States.	☐ **Your Life and Omakayas's Life** Create a PowerPoint presentation that compares Omakayas's life with your life when you were her age.	☐ **Building a Birchbark House** Make an instruction card that explains all of the steps you need to follow in order to build a birchbark house. Create a small model following all of the steps on your card.
☐ **Telling Stories** Three important oral stories were told by characters in this novel. Create a video that shares who told each story, what happened in each story, and how the story was important for Omakayas to hear.	☐ **Free Choice: The Birchbark House** (Fill out your proposal form before beginning the free choice!)	☐ **A Family Portrait** Using the clues given in the novel, make a drawing or family portrait that includes all of the members of Omakayas's family (including Old Tallow). Record the clues you found for each character on the back of your drawing.
☐ **Andeg's Journal** Pretend you are Andeg. Write six journal entries that share his thoughts on his time with Omakayas. Be sure and include his thoughts at the end of the novel.	☐ **Omakayas's Gifts** Omakayasa's family believes she has special gifts. Select quotes from the novel that support this idea. Create a mobile that shares the quotes from the novel and the gifts that each quote indicates.	☐ **Investigating Smallpox** Design a brochure that could have been used at the time to provide information on smallpox. Include how to identify the disease, how to prevent it, and its possible treatments.

Where the Mountain Meets the Moon

List Menu

A young girl named Minli lives with her family near Fruitless Mountain. After hearing stories about the Old Man of the Moon, who can answer any question he is asked, Minli embarks on a journey to find him and ask him the question that most plagues her. She meets many creatures, hears many stories, and has many adventures while trying to find the Old Man of the Moon. Will she find him? Will he be able to answer her question?

Reading Objectives Covered Through These Menus and These Activities

- Students will make predictions based on what is read.
- Students will show comprehension by retelling or acting out events in a story.
- Students will show comprehension by summarizing a story.
- Students will analyze characters, their relationships, and their importance in the story.
- Students will recognize and analyze story plot and problem resolution.

Writing Objectives Covered Through These Menus and These Activities

- Students will write to express their feelings, reflect, inform, explain, describe, entertain, or narrate.

Materials Needed by Students for Completion

- *Where the Mountain Meets the Moon* by Grace Lin
- Poster board or large white paper
- Magazines (for collages)
- Blank index cards (for mobiles, concentration cards ▲ ●)
- Coat hangers (for mobiles)
- String (for mobiles)
- Recycled materials (for models)
- Materials for board games (folders, colored cards, etc.)
- Scrapbooking materials
- Microsoft PowerPoint or other slideshow software ■
- DVD or VHS recorder (for videos)

Special Notes on the Modifications of These Menus

- Because a list menu is a point-based menu, it is easy to provide additional modifications by simply changing the point goal for those students who need it. The bottom of the menu has a short contract that can be used to record any changes. The two-page format of the triangle and circle menu also allow for additional modification by mixing and matching the pages. The front of each of these two-page menus has the lower and middle-level activities, while the second page has the higher level activities and contract. Additional modifications can be made by using the first page from the circle menu with the second page from the triangle menu. This will allow students a little more flexibility when approaching the higher level activities.

Special Notes on the Use of These Menus

- These menus give students the opportunity to create a video. Although students enjoy producing their own videos, there often are difficulties obtaining the equipment and scheduling the use of a video recorder. This activity can be modified by allowing students to act out the product (like a play) or, if students have the technology, allowing them to produce a webcam version of their product.
- This menu asks students to use recycled materials to create their model. This does not mean only plastic and paper; instead, students should focus on using materials in new ways. It works well if a box is started for "recycled" contributions at the beginning of the school year. That way, students always have access to these types of materials.

Time Frame

- 1–2 weeks—Students are given a menu as the reading of the story is started, and the guidelines and point expectations are discussed. Students usually will need to earn 100 points for 100%, although there is an opportunity for extra credit if the teacher would like to use another target number. Because this menu covers the story in depth, the teacher will go over all of the options for work being covered and have students place check marks in the boxes next to the activities they are most interested in completing. Teachers will need to set aside a few moments to sign the agreement at the bottom of the page with each student. As reading continues, activities are completed by students and submitted to the teacher for grading.
- 1–2 days—The teacher chooses an activity or product from an objective to use with the entire class during that lesson time.

Suggested Forms

- All-purpose rubric
- Student presentation rubric
- Proposal form for point-based products

Name: _____

Where the Mountain Meets the Moon: Side 1

Guidelines:

1. You may complete as many of the activities listed within the time period.
2. You may choose any combination of activities.
3. Your goal is 100 points. You may earn up to _____ points extra credit.
4. You may be as creative as you like within the guidelines listed below.
5. You must show your plan to your teacher by _____.
6. Activities may be turned in at any time during the working time period. They will be graded and recorded on this sheet as you continue to work, so keep it safe!

Plan to Do	Activity to Complete (Side 1: 10–25 points)	Point Value	Date Completed	Points Earned
	Make a drawing to show what it looks like where Minli lives.	10		
	Design a collage of at least eight challenging words found in the story. Label each word with a brief definition.	10		
	Create a picture dictionary for at least five Chinese characters that are important to this story.	15		
	Make a set of concentration cards to match the main characters from the stories Minli hears with what happens in each story.	15		
	Build a mobile that shows at least three of the animals Minli interacts with in the story. Include information about each animal and how it helps Minli on her journey.	20		
	Create a worksheet with at least 8 questions about the story. Be sure and include an answer key!	20		
	Draw a map that could help others from Fruitless Mountain find where the Old Man of the Moon lives.	25		
	The word *fortune* can mean different things. Considering what Minli discovers, tell a story about your fortune.	25		
	Total number of points you are planning to earn from Side 1.	**Total points earned from Side 1:**		

Where the Mountain Meets the Moon: Side 2

Guidelines:

1. You may complete as many of the activities listed within the time period.
2. You may choose any combination of activities.
3. Your goal is 100 points. You may earn up to _____ points extra credit.
4. You may be as creative as you like within the guidelines listed below.
5. You must show your plan to your teacher by _____.
6. Activities may be turned in at any time during the working time period. They will be graded and recorded on this sheet as you continue to work, so keep it safe!

Plan to Do	Activity to Complete (Side 2: 25–40 points)	Point Value	Date Completed	Points Earned
	Design a board game in which players experience the same adventures as Minli.	25		
	Using a Venn diagram, compare the buffalo boy's life with Minli's life.	25		
	Minli is told many stories by her father and by others during her adventure. Select the one you like best and dramatically retell the story.	25		
	Of all the stories Minli was told, which one helped her most on her quest? Record a video of yourself telling this story.	30		
	Using all of the descriptions in the book, make a model of Dragon.	30		
	Create a scrapbook to document Minli's journey to find the Old Man of the Moon.	35		
	Keep a diary for at least 4 days of Minli's journey. Be sure and include the people that she meets as well as her thoughts on any stories that she hears.	35		
	Write a new ending to the story based on Minli asking a different question of the Old Man of the Moon.	40		
	Free choice: Submit your free choice proposal form for a product of your choice.			
	Total number of points you are planning to earn from Side 1.	**Total points earned from Side 1:**		
	Total number of points you are planning to earn from Side 2.	**Total points earned from Side 2:**		
		Grand Total (/100)		

I am planning to complete _____ activities that could earn up to a total of _____ points.

Teacher's initials _____ Student's signature _____

Name: _____

Where the Mountain Meets the Moon: Side 1

Guidelines:

1. You may complete as many of the activities listed within the time period.
2. You may choose any combination of activities.
3. Your goal is 100 points. You may earn up to _____ points extra credit.
4. You may be as creative as you like within the guidelines listed below.
5. You must show your plan to your teacher by _____.
6. Activities may be turned in at any time during the working time period. They will be graded and recorded on this sheet as you continue to work, so keep it safe!

Plan to Do	Activity to Complete (Side 1: 10–20 points)	Point Value	Date Completed	Points Earned
	Make a drawing to show what it looks like where Minli lives.	10		
	Create a worksheet with at least 10 questions about the story. Be sure and include an answer key!	10		
	Design a collage of at least 10 challenging words found in the story. Label each word with its page number and a brief definition.	10		
	Build a mobile that shows at least five of the animals Minli interacts with in the story. Include information about each animal and how it helps Minli on her journey.	15		
	Create a picture dictionary for at least eight Chinese characters that are important to this story.	15		
	Make a set of concentration cards to match the main characters from the stories Minli hears with what happens in each story.	15		
	The word *fortune* can mean different things. Considering what Minli discovers, make a poster of your fortune.	15		
	Draw a map that could help others from Fruitless Mountain find where the Old Man of the Moon lives.	20		
	Total number of points you are planning to earn from Side 1.		**Total points earned from Side 1:**	

Name: _____ ●

Where the Mountain Meets the Moon: Side 2

Guidelines:

1. You may complete as many of the activities listed within the time period.
2. You may choose any combination of activities.
3. Your goal is 100 points. You may earn up to _____ points extra credit.
4. You may be as creative as you like within the guidelines listed below.
5. You must show your plan to your teacher by _____.
6. Activities may be turned in at any time during the working time period. They will be graded and recorded on this sheet as you continue to work, so keep it safe!

Plan to Do	Activity to Complete (Side 2: 25–35 points)	Point Value	Date Completed	Points Earned
	Design a board game in which players experience the same adventures as Minli.	25		
	Minli is told many stories by her father and by others during her adventure. Select the one you like best and create a children's book from the story.	25		
	Using a Venn diagram, compare the buffalo boy's life with Minli's life.	25		
	Using all of the descriptions in the book, make a model of Dragon.	25		
	Create a scrapbook to document Minli's journey to find the Old Man of the Moon.	30		
	Keep a diary for at least 5 days of Minli's journey. Be sure and include the people that she meets as well as her thoughts on any stories that she hears.	30		
	Of all the stories Minli was told, which one helped her most on her quest? Record a video of yourself telling this story.	30		
	Create a PowerPoint presentation that explains the importance peaches play throughout the story. Be sure and include as many examples as you can!	35		
	Write a new ending to the story based on Minli asking a different question of the Old Man of the Moon.	35		
	Free choice: Submit your free choice proposal form for a product of your choice.			
	Total number of points you are planning to earn from Side 1.	**Total points earned from Side 1:**		
	Total number of points you are planning to earn from Side 2.	**Total points earned from Side 2:**		
		Grand Total (/100)		

I am planning to complete _____ activities that could earn up to a total of _____ points.

Teacher's initials _____ Student's signature _____

Name: _____

Where the Mountain Meets the Moon

Guidelines:

1. You may complete as many of the activities listed within the time period.
2. You may choose any combination of activities.
3. Your goal is 100 points. You may earn up to _____ points extra credit.
4. You may be as creative as you like within the guidelines listed below.
5. You must show your plan to your teacher by _____.
6. Activities may be turned in at any time during the working time period. They will be graded and recorded on this sheet as you continue to work, so keep it safe!

Plan to Do	Activity to Complete	Point Value	Date Completed	Points Earned
	Make a collage of at least 15 challenging words found in the story. Label each word with its page number and a brief definition.	10		
	Create a set of concentration cards to match the main characters from the stories Minli hears with what happens in each story.	10		
	Draw a picture dictionary for at least 10 Chinese characters that are important to this story.	15		
	Draw a map that could help others from Fruitless Mountain find where the Old Man of the Moon lives.	15		
	Build a mobile that shows all of the animals Minli interacts with in the story. Include information about each and how it helps Minli on her journey.	15		
	The word *fortune* can mean different things. Considering what Minli discovers, make a poster of your fortune.	15		
	Using a Venn diagram, compare the buffalo boy's life with Minli's life.	20		
	Using all of the descriptions in the book, make a model of Dragon.	20		
	Why do you think the Old Man of the Moon is so difficult to find? Write a newspaper article on this man and all of the things he has accomplished in the past.	20		
	Design a board game in which players experience the same adventures as Minli.	20		
	Create a scrapbook to document Minli's journey to find the Old Man of the Moon.	25		
	Family is very important to Minli. Write a letter to a family member explaining how important he or she is to you.	25		
	Minli is told many stories by her father and by others during her adventure. Select the one you like best and create a children's book from the story.	25		
	Create a PowerPoint presentation that explains the importance peaches play throughout the story. Be sure and include as many examples as you can!	30		
	Keep a diary for at least 6 days of Minli's journey. Be sure and include the people that she meets as well as her thoughts on any stories which she hears.	30		
	Of all the stories Minli was told, which one helped her most on her quest? Record a video of yourself telling this story.	30		
	Write a new ending to the story based on Minli asking a different question of the Old Man of the Moon.	30		
	Free choice: Submit your free choice proposal form for a product of your choice.			
	Total number of points you are planning to earn.		**Total points earned:**	

I am planning to complete _____ activities that could earn up to a total of _____ points.

Teacher's initials _____ Student's signature _____

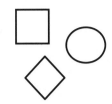

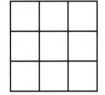

Tuck Everlasting

Three Shape Menu ▲
and Tic-Tac-Toe Menu ● ■

In *Tuck Everlasting*, Winnie is an overprotected young lady who befriends the Tuck family. Winnie soon discovers that the Tucks have a unique family secret. They have a special spring on the property that gives eternal life; the drinker will never age or die. The Tucks have developed ways to deal with this situation, but when a man comes to try and take the water to sell, Mae Tuck kills the man. Mae cannot die, nor will she age, and if she is put in jail, then the Tucks' secret will be discovered. What can be done?

Reading Objectives Covered Through These Menus and These Activities

- Students will make and explain inferences made from the story.
- Students will make predictions based on what is read.
- Students will show comprehension by retelling or acting out events in a story.
- Students will show comprehension by summarizing a story.
- Students will represent textual evidence by using story maps.
- Students will analyze characters, their relationships, and their importance in the story.
- Students will recognize and analyze story plot and problem resolution.

Writing Objectives Covered Through These Menus and These Activities

- Students will write to express their feelings, reflect, inform, explain, describe, entertain, or narrate.
- Students will exhibit voice in their writing.

Materials Needed by Students for Completion

- *Tuck Everlasting* by Natalie Babbitt
- Poster board or large white paper
- *Tuck Everlasting* cube template ● ■
- DVD or VHS recorder (for video messages ▲, commercials ■)
- Materials for board games (folders, colored cards, etc.) ● ■
- Microsoft PowerPoint or other slideshow software ■
- Magazines (for collages) ●
- Story map ▲ ■
- Blank index cards (for trading cards) ▲

Special Notes on the Modifications of These Menus

- This topic has two different menu formats: the Three Shape menu (▲) and Tic-Tac-Toe (● ■) menu. The Three Shape menu is specifically selected for the triangle option, as it easily allows the menu to be broken into manageable bits; the three shapes visually separate the page, making it less daunting for special needs students. The space between the three shapes makes it easy for the teacher to cut the menu as needed based on the comfort level of the students. If it is the first time choice is being introduced, then the children may receive only the strip of the top row or square options. Then, when they have finished one of those options, they can receive a strip of circles and finally, the enrichment-level diamond activities. After students have grown more accustomed to making choices, the menu might be cut just once after the circles, so students can select a square and a circle and submit them to the teacher. Then, they can choose from the diamond strip they receive. The ultimate goal would be for students to have all nine options at once and not be overwhelmed.

Special Notes on the Use of These Menus

- These menus give students the opportunity to create a video message and commercial. Although students enjoy producing their own videos, there often are difficulties obtaining the equipment and scheduling the use of a video recorder. These activities can be modified by allowing students to act out the products (like a play) or, if students have the technology, allowing them to produce a webcam version of their products.

Time Frame

- 1–3 weeks—Students are given a menu as the story or novel is started. As reading progresses and the teacher presents lessons throughout the week, he or she should refer back to the menu options associated with that content. The teacher will go over all of the options for the story and have students indicate the activities they are most interested in completing. When using the Tic-Tac-Toe format, students should complete a column or a row. If they are using the Three Shape format, students will be completing an activity for each of the three shapes. When students complete these patterns, they have completed one activity from each content area, learning style, or level of Bloom's revised taxonomy, depending on the design of the menu.
- 1 week—At the start of the unit, the teacher chooses the three activities he or she feels are most valuable for students. Stations can be set up in the classroom. These three activities are available for student choice throughout the week as regular instruction takes place.

- 1–2 days—The teacher chooses an activity from the menus to use with the entire class.

Suggested Forms

- All-purpose rubric
- Student presentation rubric
- Free-choice proposal form

Tuck Everlasting

Directions: Circle one choice from each group of shapes. Color in the shape after you have finished it. All products are due by : _____.

Tuck Everlasting has many important events. Complete a story map for this novel.

Create a set of trading cards with one card for each member of Winnie's family and one card for each member of the Tuck family.

Pretend that you are Winnie and you want to remember of all of your adventures. Make a drawing of the most important thing that has happened to you.

Winnie made her decision about drinking from the spring. Do you think it was the right decision? Record a video message to Winnie sharing your feelings.

Choose the most important scene in the book and change it into a skit. With the help of your classmates, perform this scene for your classmates.

After reading the epilogue, write your own story that tells what may have happened after the story ended.

The water from the spring could be very valuable. Create an advertisement that the man in the yellow suit may have used to sell the spring water if he had been able to obtain it.

Create a brochure that shares information on the fountain of youth and all of the reasons why someone might want to find it.

Write and sing a song about the dangers or benefits of drinking the Tuck's spring water.

Name: _____   ●

Tuck Everlasting

Directions: Check the boxes you plan to complete. They should form a tic-tac-toe across or down. All products are due by: _____.

☐ **Analyzing the Novel** *Tuck Everlasting* has many different facets. Complete the cube for this novel.	☐ **Expressing Your Opinion** Winnie is getting ready to make her decision about drinking from the spring. Create a poster to show her what you believe her decision should be and why.	☐ **Selling the Water** The water from the spring could be very valuable. Create an advertisement that the man in the yellow suit may have used to sell the spring water if he had been able to obtain it.
☐ **Reenact a Scene** Choose the most important scene in the book and change it into a skit. With the help of your classmates, perform this scene for your classmates.	☐ **Free Choice:** *Tuck Everlasting* (Fill out your proposal form before beginning the free choice!)	☐ **Comparing Families** Winnie found a lot of differences between her family and the Tucks. Create a collage that shows how her family and the Tucks are both alike and different. Label each picture with the family it represents.
☐ **The Fountain of Youth** Throughout history, people have searched for the fountain of youth. Research one of these people and prepare a PowerPoint presentation about where his or her searches led.	☐ **Experiencing** *Tuck Everlasting* Design a board game in which players go through the book and answer questions about the literary elements found in *Tuck Everlasting*.	☐ **Create Your Own Ending** Although the author provides an epilogue to the novel, write your own story that tells what may have happened after the story ended.

Name: _____ ■

Tuck Everlasting

Directions: Check the boxes you plan to complete. They should form a tic-tac-toe across or down. All products are due by: _____.

☐ **Analyzing the Novel**	☐ **Expressing Your Opinion**	☐ **Selling the Water**
Tuck Everlasting has many different facets. Complete a story map and the cube for this novel.	Winnie made her decision about drinking from the spring. Do you think it was the right deicision? Write a letter to Winnie explaining whether you agree or disagree with her actions and why.	The water from the spring could be very valuable. Create a commercial the man in the yellow suit may have used to sell the spring water if he had been able to obtain it.
☐ **Reenact a Scene**	☐ **Free Choice:** *Tuck Everlasting* (Fill out your proposal form before beginning the free choice!)	☐ **Comparing Families**
Choose the most important scene in the book and change it into a skit. With the help of your classmates, perform this scene for your classmates.		Winnie found a lot of differences between her family and the Tucks. Create a Venn diagram to compare the two families.
☐ **Consider the Title**	☐ **Experiencing** *Tuck Everlasting*	☐ **Create Your Own Ending**
Consider the title of this story. What other meaning could it have had? Write a children's book with the same title, but a different story.	Design a board game in which players are able to face the same decisions and have the same experiences as the characters in *Tuck Everlasting*.	Although the author provides an epilogue to the novel, create your own version of what may have happened after the story ended.

Tuck Everlasting Cube

Complete the cube for *Tuck Everlasting*. Respond to the questions on each side to analyze this novel in depth.

Use this pattern or create your own cube.

What was the problem faced in this novel?

Which character is most like you? Why?

Describe the setting of the novel.

Which character was most important to the novel? Why?

What would be another good name for this novel? Why?

What was your favorite quote in the novel? Why?

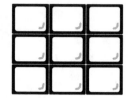

Alice's Adventures in Wonderland

Game Show Menus

When Alice sees a white rabbit run past her, she has no idea of all the adventures that await her when she decides to follow him down the rabbit hole. She will eat and drink foods with unexpected results, crash a tea party, and even attend a very important trial. With each new twist and turn, Alice begins to wonder if she will ever find her way home.

Reading Objectives Covered Through These Menus and These Activities

- Students will represent textual evidence and use it to prove conclusions.
- Students will compare one literary work with another.
- Students will interpret figurative language and multiple meaning words.
- Students will make and explain inferences made from the story.
- Students will make predictions based on what is read.
- Students will show comprehension by retelling or acting out events in a story.
- Students will show comprehension by summarizing a story.
- Students will analyze characters, their relationships, and their importance in the story.
- Students will represent textual evidence by using story maps.

Writing Objectives Covered Through These Menus and These Activities

- Students will write to express their feelings, reflect, inform, explain, describe, entertain, or narrate.
- Students will write to influence or persuade.
- Students will exhibit voice in their writing.
- Students will use vivid language.

Materials Needed by Students for Completion

- *Alice's Adventures in Wonderland* by Lewis Carroll
- Poster board or large white paper
- Blank index cards (for mobiles, trading cards)
- Materials for board games (folders, colored cards, etc.) ■
- Coat hangers (for mobiles)
- String (for mobiles)
- DVD or VHS recorder (for videos, news reports ■)

- Scrapbooking materials
- Story map ▲
- Recycled materials (for dioramas) ▲
- Ruler (for comic strips) ▲

Special Notes on the Modifications of These Menus

- Because a game show menu is a point-based menu, it is easy to provide additional modifications by simply changing the point goal for those students who need it. A contract has been included on the bottom of the game show guidelines page (see p. 135) that can be used to record any changes.

Special Notes on the Use of These Menus

- These menus give students the opportunity to create a video and news report. Although students enjoy producing their own videos, there often are difficulties obtaining the equipment and scheduling the use of a video recorder. This activity can be modified by allowing students to act out their product (like a play) or, if students have the technology, allowing them to produce a webcam version of their product
- The triangle menu asks students to use recycled materials to create their diorama. This does not mean only plastic and paper; instead, students should focus on using materials in new ways. It works well if a box is started for "recycled" contributions at the beginning of the school year. That way, students always have access to these types of materials.

Time Frame

- 1–3 weeks—Students are given a menu as the novel or story unit is started and the guidelines and point expectations on the back of the menu are discussed. As reading continues throughout the unit, students and the teacher can refer back to the options associated with that aspect of the story. The teacher will go over all of the options and have students place check marks in the boxes next to the activities they are most interested in completing. As teaching continues over the next 1–3 weeks, activities are discussed, chosen, and submitted for grading.
- 1 week—At the beginning of the unit, the teacher chooses an activity from each area he or she feels would be most valuable for students. Stations can be set up in the classroom. These activities are available for student choice throughout the week as regular instruction takes place.
- 1–2 days—The teacher chooses an activity from an objective to use with the entire class during that lesson time.

Suggested Forms

- All-purpose rubric
- Student presentation rubric
- Proposal form for point-based products

Guidelines for the *Alice's Adventures in Wonderland* Game Show Menus

- You must choose at least one activity from each topic area.
- You may not do more than two activities in any one topic area for credit. (You are, of course, welcome to do more than two for your own investigation.)
- Grading will be ongoing, so turn in products as you complete them.
- All free-choice proposals must be turned in and approved *prior* to working on the free choice.
- Your goal is 120 points for a 100%. You may earn extra credit up to _____ points.
- You must show your teacher your plan for completion by: _____.

My contract:

I am planning to complete _____ activities that could earn up to a total of _____ points.

Teacher's initials _____ Student's signature _____

Alice's Adventures in Wonderland

Setting	Characters	Events	Theme	Going Further	Points for Each Level
☐ Make a poster that shows one of the settings from *Alice's Adventures in Wonderland*. (15 pts.)	☐ Create a set of trading cards for four of the characters in this story. (15 pts.)	☐ Complete a story map for *Alice's Adventures in Wonderland*. (10 pts.)	☐ Make a windowpane that shares different themes that are found in this story. (15 pts.)	☐ Design a brochure about the author and the other books he has written about Alice. (15 pts.)	**10–15 points**
☐ Make a diorama that shows a scene in which Alice is going to eat or drink something special. (20 pts.)	☐ Use a Venn diagram to compare and contrast two of the characters in the story. (25 pts.)	☐ Make a three-dimensional timeline to share the major events in the story. (20 pts.)	☐ Build a mobile for one of the themes found in this story. Be sure to include examples from the story! (25 pts.)	☐ Write a story telling what happens after Alice wakes up. (25 pts.)	**20–25 points**
☐ Draw a map of Wonderland based on Alice's description of her adventures. (30 pts.)	☐ Select one of the most interesting characters and make a video in which you share information about this character. (30 pts.)	☐ Select an event in which you would have done something differently than Alice. Make a comic strip to show what you would have changed. (30 pts.)	☐ Make a scrapbook that shows examples from the story and how they relate to one of its themes. (30 pts.)	☐ Imagine that one of the characters from Wonderland has met a character from another book you have read. Write a story about their adventure. (30 pts.)	**30 points**
Free Choice (prior approval) (10–30 pts.)	**Free Choice** (prior approval) (10–30 pts.)	**Free Choice** (prior approval) (10–30 pts.)	**Free Choice** (prior approval) (10–30 pts.)	**Free Choice** (prior approval) (10–30 pts.)	**10–30 points**
Total:	**Total:**	**Total:**	**Total:**	**Total:**	**Total Grade:**

Name: _____

Alice's Adventures in Wonderland

Setting	Characters	Events	Theme	Going Further	Points for Each Level
☐ Make a poster that shows one of the settings from *Alice's Adventures in Wonderland*. (10 pts.)	☐ Create a set of trading cards for the main characters in this story. (10 pts.)	☐ Make a three-dimensional timeline to share all of the major events in the story. (15 pts.)	☐ Make a windowpane that shares different themes that are found in this story. (10 pts.)	☐ Write a three facts and a fib about *Alice's Adventures in Wonderland*. (15 pts.)	**10–15 points**
☐ Draw a map of Wonderland based on Alice's description of her adventures. (20 pts.)	☐ Use a Venn diagram to compare and contrast yourself with one of the animals Alice meets in Wonderland. (20 pts.)	☐ Consider all of the events in the story. Which would you have done differently? Write a letter to Alice explaining how you would have done something differently. (25 pts.)	☐ Build a mobile for one of the themes found in this story. Be sure to include examples from the story! (20 pts.)	☐ Imagine that one of the characters from Wonderland has met a character from another book you have read. Write a story about their adventure. (25 pts.)	**20–25 points**
☐ Create a magazine advertisement to encourage tourists to visit Wonderland. (30 pts.)	☐ Select one of the most interesting characters and create a video in which you interview this character. (30 pts.)	☐ Perform a skit that reenacts the Knave of Hearts's trial. (30 pts.)	☐ Make a scrapbook that shows examples from the story and how they relate to one of its themes. (30 pts.)	☐ Read *Through the Looking Glass*. Compare the two books in a "book talk" video. (30 pts.)	**30 points**
Free Choice (prior approval) (10–30 pts.)	**Free Choice** (prior approval) (10–30 pts.)	**Free Choice** (prior approval) (10–30 pts.)	**Free Choice** (prior approval) (10–30 pts.)	**Free Choice** (prior approval) (10–30 pts.)	**10–30 points**
Total:	**Total:**	**Total:**	**Total:**	**Total:**	**Total Grade:**

Alice's Adventures in Wonderland

Name: _____

	Setting	Characters	Events	Theme	Going Further	Points for Each Level
	☐ Design a map of Wonderland based on Alice's description of her adventures. (15 pts.)	☐ Create a set of trading cards for all of the characters in this story. (15 pts.)	☐ Design a board game in which the players are Alice going through her many adventures in Wonderland. (15 pts.)	☐ Build a mobile for one of the themes found in this story. Be sure to include quotes from the story! (15 pts.)	☐ Write a three facts and a fib about Alice's Adventures in Wonderland. (10 pts.)	10–15 points
	☐ Create a magazine advertisement to encourage tourists to visit Wonderland. (20 pts.)	☐ Select one of the most interesting characters and create a video in which you interview this character. (25 pts.)	☐ Consider all of the events in the story. Write a letter to Alice explaining what event you would have handled differently. (20 pts.)	☐ Make a scrapbook that shows examples from the story and how they relate to one of its themes. (25 pts.)	☐ Pretend that two of the characters from Wonderland have met two characters from another book you have read. Write a story about their adventure. (25 pts.)	20–25 points
	☐ Write a "nonfiction" children's book about Wonderland and its special qualities. (30 pts.)	☐ Research when Alice's Adventures in Wonderland was written. Using a windowpane, compare the characters with famous people of the same time period. (30 pts.)	☐ Perform a news report that covers the Knave of Hearts's trial. (30 pts.)	☐ After discovering the theme of this story, select another story with the same theme and make a Venn diagram to compare the two stories. (30 pts.)	☐ Read Through the Looking Glass. Compare the two books in a "book talk" video. (30 pts.)	30 points
	Free Choice (prior approval) (10–30 pts.)	Free Choice (prior approval) (10–30 pts.)	Free Choice (prior approval) (10–30 pts.)	Free Choice (prior approval) (10–30 pts.)	Free Choice (prior approval) (10–30 pts.)	10–30 points
	Total:	Total:	Total:	Total:	Total:	Total Grade:

© Prufrock Press Inc. • *Literature for Every Learner* • *Grades 3–5*
Permission is granted to photocopy or reproduce this page for single classroom use only.

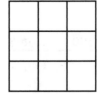

The Secret Garden

Meal Menu ▲ and Tic-Tac-Toe Menu ● ■

Mary Lennox is considered a disagreeable girl by those who know her. When her family dies from cholera, she is sent to live with a distant, sour uncle in a sprawling manor. She soon hears about a neglected hidden garden that her uncle locked up when his wife died. Mary makes it her quest to find and unlocks the secrets of the garden. In doing so, she changes not just her life, but everyone's in Misselthwaite Manor as well.

Reading Objectives Covered Through These Menus and These Activities

- Students will make and explain inferences made from the story.
- Students will show comprehension by retelling or acting out events in a story.
- Students will show comprehension by summarizing a story.
- Students will analyze characters, their relationships, and their importance in the story.
- Students will recognize and analyze story plot and problem resolution.

Writing Objectives Covered Through These Menus and These Activities

- Students will write to express their feelings, reflect, inform, explain, describe, entertain, or narrate.
- Students will exhibit voice in their writing.

Materials Needed by Students for Completion

- *The Secret Garden* by Frances Hodgson Burnett
- Poster board or large white paper
- Recycled materials (for models)
- Microsoft PowerPoint or other slideshow software ■
- DVD or VHS recorder (for videos ■, news report ▲ ●)
- Magazines (for collages) ▲
- Blank index cards (for trading cards ▲, mobiles ▲)
- Large lined index cards (for instruction cards) ▲
- Coat hangers (for mobiles) ▲
- String (for mobiles) ▲
- World map ●
- Materials for bulletin board display ■

Special Notes on the Modifications of These Menus

- This topic has two different menu formats: The Meal menu (▲) and Tic-Tac-Toe (● ■) menu. The Meal menu is specifically selected for the triangle option, as it easily allows the menu to be broken into manageable bits; the different meals separate the page, making it less daunting for special needs students. The space between the meals makes it easy for the teacher to cut the menu as needed based on the comfort level of the students. If it is the first time choice is being introduced, then the children may receive only the strip of the breakfast options. Then, when they have finished one of those options, they can receive a strip of lunches and finally, the enrichment-level dinner and dessert activities. After students have grown more accustomed to making choices, the menu might be cut just once after the lunch options, so students can select a breakfast and a lunch and submit them to the teacher. Then, they can choose from the dinner strip they receive. The ultimate goal would be for students to have all of the options at once and not be overwhelmed.

Special Notes on the Use of These Menus

- These menus give students the opportunity to create a news report or video. Although students enjoy producing their own videos, there often are difficulties obtaining the equipment and scheduling the use of a video recorder. This activity can be modified by allowing students to act out the products (like a play) or, if students have the technology, allowing them to produce a webcam version of their product.

- This menu asks students to use recycled materials to create their models. This does not mean only plastic and paper; instead, students should focus on using materials in new ways. It works well if a box is started for "recycled" contributions at the beginning of the school year. That way, students always have access to these types of materials.

- The square menu ■ allows students to create a bulletin board display. Some classrooms may only have one bulletin board, so the teacher can divide the board into sections, or additional classroom wall or hall space can be sectioned off for the creation of these displays. Students can plan their display based on the amount of space they are assigned.

Time Frame

- 1–3 weeks—Students are given a menu as the story or novel is started. As reading progresses and the teacher presents lessons throughout the week, he or she should refer back to the menu options associated with that content. The teacher will go over all of the options for that story and have students indicate the activities they are most interested in completing. If using the

Tic-Tac-Toe menu, as students choose activities, they should complete a column or a row. If using the Meal menu format, students will work to complete a choice from each meal. When students complete these patterns, they have completed one activity from each content area, learning style, or level of Bloom's revised taxonomy, depending on the format of the menu.

- 1 week—At the start of the unit, the teacher chooses the three activities he or she feels are most valuable for students. Stations can be set up in the classroom. These three activities are available for student choice throughout the week as regular instruction takes place.
- 1–2 days—The teacher chooses an activity from the menus to use with the entire class.

Suggested Forms

- All-purpose rubric
- Student presentation rubric
- Free-choice proposal form

The Secret Garden

Directions: Choose one activity each for breakfast, lunch, and dinner. Dessert is an activity you can choose to do after you have finished your other meals. All products must be completed by: _____.

Breakfast

❑ Design a collage of words that are used to describe Mary in the book. Label each word with who said it about her.

❑ Make a set of five trading cards for the main characters in *The Secret Garden*.

❑ Create your own book cover for *The Secret Garden* that features two important characters from the story.

Lunch

❑ Build a model of the secret garden and all of its plants once Mary has been working in it.

❑ Make a set of drawings that show how the secret garden has changed throughout the story.

❑ Write an instruction card that tells the steps you need to follow to tend to a garden.

Dinner

❑ Research cholera and prepare a poster about the disease.

❑ The robin was important to the story. Make a mobile that shares important information about this type of bird.

❑ Use a Venn diagram to compare and contrast life in England and India.

Dessert

❑ The garden seems magical in many ways. Record a news report that tells about the secret garden and people who have helped make it beautiful again.

❑ Free choice: Submit a free choice proposal about *The Secret Garden* to your teacher for approval.

The Secret Garden

Directions: Check the boxes you plan to complete. They should form a tic-tac-toe across or down. All products are due by: _____.

☐ **Mary**	☐ **The Garden**	☐ **Events**
Design a mind map that shows the major events that take place during the story and how Mary responded to each event.	Although the secret garden is quite overgrown when it is discovered, it soon returns to its glory. Make a model of the lovely secret garden and its plants.	Mary's parents died from cholera while living in India. Research this disease and using a map, share locations where this disease is still found. Include a paragraph to explain what causes the disease.
☐ **Events** Colin feared he would become a hunchback. Prepare a poster that shows what might cause someone to look this way and how this condition would impact his or her life.	☐ **Free Choice:** *Mary and Her Experiences* (Fill out your proposal form before beginning the free choice!)	☐ **The Garden** The garden seems magical in many ways. Record a news report that tells about the secret garden and people who have helped make it beautiful again.
☐ **The Garden** Paint a mural that shows all of the changes the secret garden has experienced from the death of Mistress Craven to Master Craven's return at the end of the story.	☐ **Events** England is very different from India. Use a Venn diagram to compare and contrast how the countries are alike and different.	☐ **Mary** Write at least eight diary entries that Mary may have written at important points in the story.

The Secret Garden

Directions: Check the boxes you plan to complete. They should form a tic-tac-toe across or down. All products are due by: _____.

☐ **Mary**	☐ **The Garden**	☐ **Events**
Design a mind map that shows the major events that take place during the story and how each impacted Mary.	Research different plants that grow where you live. Make a model to show how you would design your own secret garden. Include explanations of what would be growing in each location.	Mary's parents died from cholera while living in India. Research this disease and prepare a PowerPoint presentation on its causes and what can be done to prevent it from spreading.
☐ **Events**	☐ **Free Choice: *Mary and Her Experiences*** (Fill out your proposal form before beginning the free choice!)	☐ **The Garden**
Master Craven was considered a hunchback and Colin feared he would also become a hunchback. Research what causes this condition and create a bulletin board display to share your findings.		The garden seems magical in many ways. Record a video to discuss all of the wonderful things that the secret garden brought about for the characters.
☐ **The Garden**	☐ **Events**	☐ **Mary**
Paint a mural that shows all of the changes the secret garden has experienced from the death of Mistress Craven to Master Craven's return at the end of the story.	England is very different from India. Use a Venn diagram to compare and contrast not only how the countries are alike and different but also how Mary's life is different in each place.	Consider all of the major events that took place during *The Secret Garden*. Keep a journal or diary for Mary that shares how her feelings change as the story progresses.

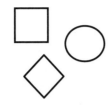

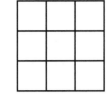

Author Study

Three Shape Menu ▲
and Tic-Tac-Toe Menu ● ■

Reading Objectives Covered Through These Menus and These Activities

- Students will compare one literary work with another.
- Students will show comprehension by retelling or acting out events in a story.
- Students will show comprehension by summarizing a story.
- Students will compare one literary genre with another.
- Students will analyze characters, their relationships, and their importance in the story.
- Students will recognize and analyze story plot and problem resolution.

Writing Objectives Covered Through These Menus and These Activities

- Students will write to express their feelings, reflect, inform, explain, describe, entertain, or narrate.
- Students will write to influence or persuade.

Materials Needed by Students for Completion

- Poster board or large white paper
- Materials for board games (folders, colored cards, etc.)
- Recycled materials (for trophies, puppets ▲)
- DVD or VHS recorder (for videos) ● ■
- Socks (for puppets) ▲
- Paper bags (for puppets) ▲
- Scrapbooking materials ▲

Special Notes on the Modifications of These Menus

- This topic has two different menu formats: the Three Shape Menu (▲) and Tic-Tac-Toe (● ■) menu. The Three Shape menu is specifically selected for the triangle option, as it easily allows the menu to be broken into manageable bits; the three shapes visually separate the page, making it less daunting for special needs students. The space between the three shapes makes it easy for the teacher to cut the menu as needed based on the comfort level of the students. If it is the first time choice is being introduced, then the children may receive only the strip of the top row or square options. Then, when they have finished one of those options, they can receive a strip of circles and finally, the enrichment-level diamond activities. After students have grown more accustomed to making choices, the menu might be cut just once after the circles, so students can select a square and a circle and submit them to the teacher. Then, they can choose from the diamond strip they receive. The ultimate goal would be for students to have all nine options at once and not be overwhelmed.

Special Notes on the Use of These Menus

- The circle and square ● ■ menus give students the opportunity to create videos. Although students enjoy producing their own videos, there often are difficulties obtaining the equipment and scheduling the use of a video recorder. This activity can be modified by allowing students to act out the video (like a play) or, if students have the technology, allowing them to produce a webcam version of their product.
- This menu asks students to use recycled materials to create their puppets ▲ and trophies. This does not mean only plastic and paper; instead, students should focus on using materials in new ways. It works well if a box is started for "recycled" contributions at the beginning of the school year. That way, students always have access to these types of materials.

Time Frame

- 1–3 weeks—Students are given a menu as the story or novel is started. As reading progresses and the teacher presents lessons throughout the week, he or she should refer back to the menu options associated with that content. The teacher will go over all of the options for the story and have students indicate the activities they are most interested in completing. When using the Tic-Tac-Toe format, students should complete a column or a row. If they are using the Three Shape format, students will be completing an activity for each of the three shapes. When students complete these patterns, they have completed one activity from each content area, learning style, or level of Bloom's revised taxonomy, depending on the design of the menu.
- 1 week—At the start of the unit, the teacher chooses the three activities he or she feels are most valuable for students. Stations can be set up in the classroom. These three activities are available for student choice throughout the week as regular instruction takes place.
- 1–2 days—The teacher chooses an activity from the menus to use with the entire class.

Suggested Forms

- All-purpose rubric
- Student presentation rubric
- Free-choice proposal form

Author Study

Directions: Circle one choice from each group of shapes. Color in the shape after you have finished it. All products are due by : _____.

Create a three-dimensional time line with at least five significant events in your author's life that led to his or her career in writing.

Design a poster to share important information about your author and his or her life.

Come to school as your author and talk about your life and the stories you have written.

Turn one of your author's stories into a puppet show or skit. Present your creation.

Design a board game based on one of the adventures found in one of your author's stories.

Draw an advertisement to convince your classmates to read one of your author's stories.

Create a scrapbook of book covers that your author might enjoy reading. Include a sentence to explain why your author might like each book.

One of the stories or books your author has written has been nominated for the Best Book of the Year Award. Create a trophy for the award.

Pretend that one of the stories your author has written is being turned into a musical. Choose a song one of the characters might sing during the musical version of the story.

Author Study

Directions: Check the boxes you plan to complete. They should form a tic-tac-toe across or down. All products are due by: _____.

☐ **Author's Life**	☐ **Author's Works**	☐ **Having Fun With an Author**
Create a three-dimensional timeline with at least six significant events in your author's life that led to his or her career in writing.	Write an original play in which two characters from your story have a new adventure.	Make an acrostic using your author's first and last name. For each letter, record a phrase or word that shares special information about your author.
☐ **Having Fun With an Author** Pretend that one of the stories your author has written is being turned into a musical. Choose three songs (do not have to be original) that your characters might sing during the musical version of the story.	☐ **Free Choice: *Author's Life*** (Fill out your proposal form before beginning the free choice!)	☐ **Author's Works** Design a board game in which the players are characters in one of your author's books. Be sure to include all of the adventures your characters experience.
☐ **Author's Works** Find three classmates who have read at least one story or book by your author. Record a video in which they share their thoughts on the different works.	☐ **Having Fun With an Author** One of the stories or books your author has written has been nominated for the Best Book of the Year Award. Create a trophy for the award.	☐ **Author's Life** Come to school as your author and talk about your life and why you wanted to become a writer.

Name: _____ ■

Author Study

Directions: Check the boxes you plan to complete. They should form a tic-tac-toe across or down. All products are due by: _____.

☐ **Author's Life**	☐ **Author's Works**	☐ **Having Fun With an Author**
Create a three-dimensional time line with at least 10 significant events in your author's life that led to his or her career in writing.	Write an original play in which at least two different characters from two different books by your author meet and have an adventure.	Considering the characters and types of stories your author writes, design a bumper sticker that your author may put on his or her car.
☐ **Having Fun With an Author** Pretend that one of the stories your author has written is being turned into a musical. Write two original songs that the characters might sing during the musical version of the story.	☐ **Free Choice: Author's Life** (Fill out your proposal form before beginning the free choice!)	☐ **Author's Works** Design a board game in which the players are characters in one of your author's books. Be sure to include at least one adventure that the author did not include in his or her story but could have happened.
☐ **Author's Works** Find three classmates who have read at least one story or book by your author. Record a video in which they share their thoughts on the different works.	☐ **Having Fun With an Author** One of the stories or books your author has written has been nominated for a special award. What award will the author be receiving? Create a trophy for the award.	☐ **Author's Life** Come to school as your author. Talk about your life, the favorite book that you have written, and why you wanted to become a writer.

CHAPTER 6

Poetry

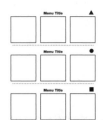

"Casey at the Bat"

Poetry Shape Menu

Reading Objectives Covered Through This Menu and These Activities

- Students will interpret figurative language and multiple meaning words.
- Students will make predictions based on what is read.
- Students will use resources and references to build meaning.

Writing Objectives Covered Through This Menu and These Activities

- Students will write to express their feelings, reflect, inform, explain, describe, entertain, or narrate.
- Students will use vivid language.

Materials Needed by Students for Completion

- "Casey at the Bat" by Ernest Lawrence Thayer, see page 154
- Poster board or large white paper
- Story map ▲
- Recycled materials (for dioramas) ▲
- DVD or VHS recorder (for news reports) ■

Special Notes on the Modifications of This Menu

- This menu is unique from the others, as teachers can select the number of choices based on the amount of time they plan to spend processing a particular poem. This menu is divided into three sections; the top ▲ or triangle section has activities with the most modifications, the middle ● or circle section has activities with minor modifications, and the lower ■ or square section has activities that offer the most extension. If the goal is to have students create one product for the poem, then the teacher can provide each student with a strip of an appropriate level of options. For a more in-depth study, the teacher can provide the entire menu and students select one option from each section of the menu.

Special Notes on the Use of This Menu

- The square ■ strip of this menu gives students the opportunity to create a news report. Although students enjoy producing their own videos, there often are difficulties obtaining the equipment and scheduling the use of a video recorder. This activity can be modified by allowing students to act out the news report (like a play) or, if students have the technology, allowing them to produce a webcam version of their product.

- The triangle ▲ strip of this menu asks students to use recycled materials to create their dioramas. This does not mean only plastic and paper; instead, students should focus on using materials in new ways. It works well if a box is started for "recycled" contributions at the beginning of the school year. That way, students always have access to these types of materials.

Time Frame

- 1 week—Students are given the menu before the poem is read. The teacher will go over all of the options for the menu and have students indicate each option that represents the activity they are most interested in completing. The teacher may assign the menu as independent work or choose to allow students time to work after their other work is finished.
- 1–2 days—The teacher chooses a strip for each student to complete based on his or her specific needs. The student selects one of the activities on the strip and works on it for independent practice.

Suggested Forms

- All-purpose rubric
- Student presentation rubric

Casey at the Bat

by ErnLawrence Thayer

The outlook wasn't brilliant for the Mudville nine that day;
The score stood four to two, with but one inning more to play,
And then when Cooney died at first, and Barrows did the same,
A pall-like silence fell upon the patrons of the game.

A straggling few got up to go in deep despair. The rest
Clung to that hope which springs eternal in the human breast;
They thought, "If only Casey could but get a whack at that—
We'd put up even money now, with Casey at the bat."

But Flynn preceded Casey, as did also Jimmy Blake,
And the former was a hoodoo, while the latter was a cake;
So upon that stricken multitude grim melancholy sat,
For there seemed but little chance of Casey getting to the bat.

But Flynn let drive a single, to the wonderment of all,
And Blake, the much despisèd, tore the cover off the ball;
And when the dust had lifted, and men saw what had occurred,
There was Jimmy safe at second and Flynn a-hugging third.

Then from five thousand throats and more there rose a lusty yell;
It rumbled through the valley, it rattled in the dell;
It pounded on the mountain and recoiled upon the flat,
For Casey, mighty Casey, was advancing to the bat.

There was ease in Casey's manner as he stepped into his place;
There was pride in Casey's bearing and a smile lit Casey's face.
And when, responding to the cheers, he lightly doffed his hat,
No stranger in the crowd could doubt 'twas Casey at the bat.

Ten thousand eyes were on him as he rubbed his hands with dirt;
Five thousand tongues applauded when he wiped them on his shirt;
Then while the writhing pitcher ground the ball into his hip,
Defiance flashed in Casey's eye, a sneer curled Casey's lip.

And now the leather-covered sphere came hurtling through the air,
And Casey stood a-watching it in haughty grandeur there.

Close by the sturdy batsman the ball unheeded sped—
"That ain't my style," said Casey. "Strike one!" the umpire said.

From the benches, black with people, there went up a muffled roar,
Like the beating of the storm-waves on a stern and distant shore;
"Kill him! Kill the umpire!" shouted some one on the stand;
And it's likely they'd have killed him had not Casey raised his hand.

With a smile of Christian charity great Casey's visage shone;
He stilled the rising tumult; he bade the game go on;
He signaled to the pitcher, and once more the dun sphere flew;
But Casey still ignored it, and the umpire said, "Strike two!"

"Fraud!" cried the maddened thousands, and echo answered "Fraud!"
But one scornful look from Casey and the audience was awed.
They saw his face grow stern and cold, they saw his muscles strain,
And they knew that Casey wouldn't let that ball go by again.

The sneer has fled from Casey's lip, his teeth are clenched in hate;
He pounds with cruel violence his bat upon the plate.
And now the pitcher holds the ball, and now he lets it go.
And now the air is shattered by the force of Casey's blow.

Oh, somewhere in this favored land the sun is shining bright;
The band is playing somewhere, and somewhere hearts are light,
And somewhere men are laughing, and little children shout;
But there is no joy in Mudville—great Casey has struck out.

"Casey at the Bat"

Directions: Select one of the following options.

▲

Create a picture dictionary for 10 of the unusual words in the poem.

This poem tells a story. Complete a basic story map for "Casey at the Bat."

Create a diorama of the scene in "Casey at the Bat."

- -

"Casey at the Bat"

Directions: Select one of the following options.

●

Design a baseball uniform that Casey's team may have worn.

Turn "Casey at the Bat" into a skit and perform it for your classmates. Be sure and come in costume with any props you may need!

Create an illustrated version of "Casey at the Bat" by turning the poem into a children's book.

- -

"Casey at the Bat"

Directions: Select one of the following options.

■

Select three different examples of creative language that would be funny if taken literally (for example, "the latter was a cake") and draw three cartoons to show the literal meaning of each as well as what it means in the poem.

Considering what happened to Casey, will the fans still love him? Record a news report that details what took place during the game. Be sure to interview some of Casey's fans for their thoughts on the game.

Is Casey a real person? Was this a real game? Research who the poet was writing about and discover if this poem represents a real game. Present your findings through a product of your choice.

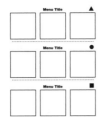

"A Bird Came Down the Walk"

Poetry Shape Menu

Reading Objectives Covered Through This Menu and These Activities

- Students will interpret figurative language and multiple meaning words.
- Students will make predictions based on what is read.
- Students will use resources and references to build meaning.

Writing Objectives Covered Through This Menu and These Activities

- Students will write to express their feelings, reflect, inform, explain, describe, entertain, or narrate.
- Students will use vivid language.

Materials Needed by Students for Completion

- "A Bird Came Down the Walk" by Emily Dickinson, see page 159
- Poster board or large white paper
- "A Bird Came Down the Walk" Cube template ▲
- Coat hangers (for mobiles) ■
- String (for mobiles) ■
- Blank index cards (for mobiles) ■
- Large lined index cards (for instruction cards) ■
- Socks (for puppets) ●
- Paper bags (for puppets) ●
- Recycled materials (for puppets) ●

Special Notes on the Modifications of This Menu

- This menu is unique from the others, as teachers can select the number of choices based on the amount of time they plan to spend processing a particular poem. This menu is divided into three sections; the top ▲ or triangle section has activities with the most modifications, the middle ● or circle section has activities with minor modifications, and the lower ■ or square section has activities that offer the most extension. If the goal is to have students create one product for the poem, then the teacher can provide each student with a strip of an appropriate level of options. For a more in-depth study, the teacher can provide the entire menu and students select one option from each section of the menu.

Special Notes on the Use of This Menu

- The circle ● menu asks students to use recycled materials to create their puppets. This does not mean only plastic and paper; instead, students should focus on using materials in new ways. It works well if a box is started for "recycled" contributions at the beginning of the school year. That way, students always have access to these types of materials.

Time Frame

- 1 week—Students are given the menu before the poem is read. The teacher will go over all of the options for the menu and have students indicate each option that represents the activity they are most interested in completing. The teacher may assign the menu as independent work or choose to allow students time to work after other work is finished.
- 1–2 days—The teacher chooses a strip for each student to complete based on his or her specific needs. The student selects one of the activities on the strip and works on it for independent practice.

Suggested Forms

- All-purpose rubric

"A Bird Came Down the Walk"

by Emily Dickinson

A Bird came down the Walk—
He did not know I saw—
He bit an Angleworm in halves
And ate the fellow, raw,

And then he drank a Dew
From a convenient Grass—
And then hopped sidewise to the Wall
To let a Beetle pass—

He glanced with rapid eyes
That hurried all around—
They looked like frightened Beads, I thought—
He stirred his Velvet Head

Like one in danger, Cautious,
I offered him a Crumb
And he unrolled his feathers
And rowed him softer home—

Than Oars divide the Ocean,
Too silver for a seam—
Or Butterflies, off Banks of Noon
Leap, plashless as they swim.

Name: _____

"A Bird Came Down the Walk"

Directions: Select one of the following options.　　　　　▲

Create a drawing to show what happens in the poem.

Complete the product cube for "A Bird Came Down the Walk."

Make a windowpane for six "new to you" words used in the poem.

- -

"A Bird Came Down the Walk"

Directions: Select one of the following options.　　　　　●

Create a puppet to represent what the bird might look like in this poem.

Turn this poem into a children's book with illustrations. Read your book to your classmates.

Create a flipbook with five sections (one for each stanza of the poem) and write a question about each inside.

- -

"A Bird Came Down the Walk"

Directions: Select one of the following options.　　　　　■

Consider how flying is compared to swimming. Design a mobile with examples of other such comparisons.

Think about how Emily Dickinson writes her poems. Make an instruction card that shares the steps for writing a good poem.

Select another poem by Emily Dickinson and use a Venn diagram to compare and contrast them.

"A Bird Came Down the Walk" Cube ▲

Fill in each side of the cube with the answers to the Five Ws (and one H). Use this pattern or create your own cube. You may choose to put questions or statements on each side of your cube.

Who are the characters in the poem?

What happens in the poem?

Where does the poem take place?

When do you think the poem takes place?

Why does the bird fly away?

How does the author feel about the bird?

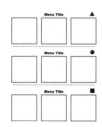

"Dust of Snow"

Poetry Shape Menu

Reading Objectives Covered Through This Menu and These Activities

- Students will interpret figurative language and multiple meaning words.
- Students will make predictions based on what is read.
- Students will use resources and references to build meaning.

Writing Objectives Covered Through This Menu and These Activities

- Students will write to express their feelings, reflect, inform, explain, describe, entertain, or narrate.
- Students will use vivid language.

Materials Needed by Students for Completion

- "Dust of Snow" by Robert Frost, see page 164
- Poster board or large white paper
- Coat hangers (for mobiles) ▲
- String (for mobiles) ▲
- Blank index cards (for mobiles) ▲
- Recycled materials (for dioramas) ▲
- Scrapbooking materials ■
- Magazines (for collages) ■

Special Notes on the Modifications of This Menu

- This menu is unique from the others, as teachers can select the number of choices based on the amount of time they plan to spend processing a particular poem. This menu is divided into three sections; the top ▲ or triangle section has activities with the most modifications, the middle ● or circle section has activities with minor modifications, and the lower ■ or square section has activities that offer the most extension. If the goal is to have students create one product for the poem, then the teacher can provide each student with a strip of an appropriate level of options. For a more in-depth study, the teacher can provide the entire menu and students select one option from each section of the menu.

Special Notes on the Use of This Menu

- The triangle menu asks students to use recycled materials to create their dioramas. This does not mean only plastic and paper; instead, students should focus on using materials in new ways. It works well if a box is started for "recycled" contributions at the beginning of the school year. That way, students always have access to these types of materials.

Time Frame

- 1 week—Students are given the menu before the poem is read. The teacher will go over all of the options for the menu and have students indicate each option that represents the activity they are most interested in completing. The teacher may assign the menu as independent work or choose to allow students time to work after other work is finished.
- 1–2 days—The teacher chooses a strip for each student to complete based on his or her specific needs. The student selects one of the activities on the strip and works on it for independent practice.

Suggested Forms

- All-purpose rubric

Dust of Snow

by Robert Frost

The way a crow
Shook down on me
The dust of snow
From a hemlock tree

Has given my heart
A change of mood
And saved some part
Of a day I had rued.

Name: _____

"Dust of Snow"

Directions: Select one of the following options.   ▲

Create a mobile with examples of these words: hemlock, crow, and dust.

Pretend you saw this happen. Retell the story for your classmates.

Build a diorama of the scene in "Dust of Snow."

"Dust of Snow"

Directions: Select one of the following options.   ●

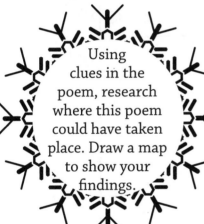

Using clues in the poem, research where this poem could have taken place. Draw a map to show your findings.

Select another poem by Robert Frost. Read the poem for your classmates and use a Venn diagram to share how it is similar and different from this one.

Design a greeting card for someone who, like the crow, has made you feel better. Consider giving him or her the card.

"Dust of Snow"

Directions: Select one of the following options.   ■

Create a scrapbook of people or activities that can quickly change your mood.

Write a story or poem to explain why the author may have been ruing the day.

Make a collage of words and ideas that you could do for others to make their day better. Do at least two of the things in your collage.

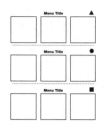

"The Echoing Green"

Poetry Shape Menu

Reading Objectives Covered Through This Menu and These Activities

- Students will interpret figurative language and multiple meaning words.
- Students will make predictions based on what is read.
- Students will use resources and references to build meaning.

Writing Objectives Covered Through This Menu and These Activities

- Students will write to express their feelings, reflect, inform, explain, describe, entertain, or narrate.
- Students will use vivid language.

Materials Needed by Students for Completion

- "The Echoing Green" by William Blake, see page 168
- "The Echoing Green" Cube template ▲
- Recycled materials (for dioramas) ▲
- Ruler (for comic strips) ▲
- Map of your city or county ●
- Poster board or large white paper ●
- Scrapbooking materials ■

Special Notes on the Modifications of This Menu

- This menu is unique from the others, as teachers can select the number of choices based on the amount of time they plan to spend processing a particular poem. This menu is divided into three sections; the top ▲ or triangle section has activities with the most modifications, the middle ● or circle section has activities with minor modifications, and the lower ■ or square section has activities that offer the most extension. If the goal is to have students create one product for the poem, then the teacher can provide each student with a strip of an appropriate level of options. For a more in-depth study, the teacher can provide the entire menu and students select one option from each section of the menu.

Special Notes on the Use of This Menu

- The triangle ▲ menu asks students to use recycled materials to create their dioramas. This does not mean only plastic and paper; instead, students should focus on using materials in new ways. It works well if a box is started for "recycled" contributions at the beginning of the school year. That way, students always have access to these types of materials.

Time Frame

- 1 week—Students are given a menu before the poem is read. The teacher will go over all of the options for the menu and have students indicate each option that represents the activity they are most interested in completing. The teacher may assign the menu as independent work or choose to allow students time to work after other work is finished.
- 1–2 days—The teacher chooses a strip for each student to complete based on his or her specific needs. The student selects one of the activities on the strip and works on it for independent practice.

Suggested Forms

- All-purpose rubric
- Student presentation rubric

The Echoing Green
by William Blake

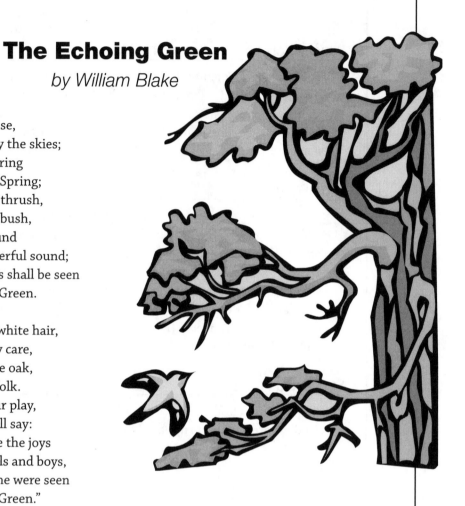

The sun does arise,
And make happy the skies;
The merry bells ring
To welcome the Spring;
The skylark and thrush,
The birds of the bush,
Sing louder around
To the bells' cheerful sound;
While our sports shall be seen
On the echoing Green.

Old John, with white hair,
Does laugh away care,
Sitting under the oak,
Among the old folk.
They laugh at our play,
And soon they all say:
"Such, such were the joys
When we all, girls and boys,
In our youth-time were seen
On the echoing Green."

Till the little ones, weary,
No more can be merry;
The sun does descend,
And our sports have an end.
Round the laps of their mothers
Many sisters and brothers,
Like birds in their nest,
Are ready for rest,
And sport no more seen
On the darkening Green.

Name: _____

"The Echoing Green"

Directions: Select one of the following options. ▲

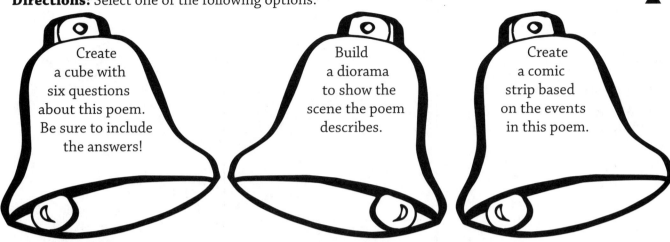

Create a cube with six questions about this poem. Be sure to include the answers!

Build a diorama to show the scene the poem describes.

Create a comic strip based on the events in this poem.

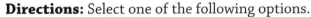

"The Echoing Green"

Directions: Select one of the following options. ●

Using a map of where you live, locate at least two areas that could be used for the same purpose as the echoing green. Share with your classmates.

Pretend you are Old John and tell a story about your time on the echoing green.

Create a poster called "Spring." Your poster should share words and pictures of what spring means to you.

"The Echoing Green"

Directions: Select one of the following options. ■

You are a newspaper reporter sent to interview Old John. Write a newspaper article based on what he tells you about his time of the echoing green.

Pretend you are the mother of one of the children on the green. Create a scrapbook to remember this special day.

Research a game the children may have played on the green that we do not play now. Teach your classmates the game.

"The Echoing Green" Cube

▲

Brainstorm six questions about this poem. Place a question on each side of the cube. Be sure to include the answers on a separate piece of paper! Use this pattern or create your own cube.

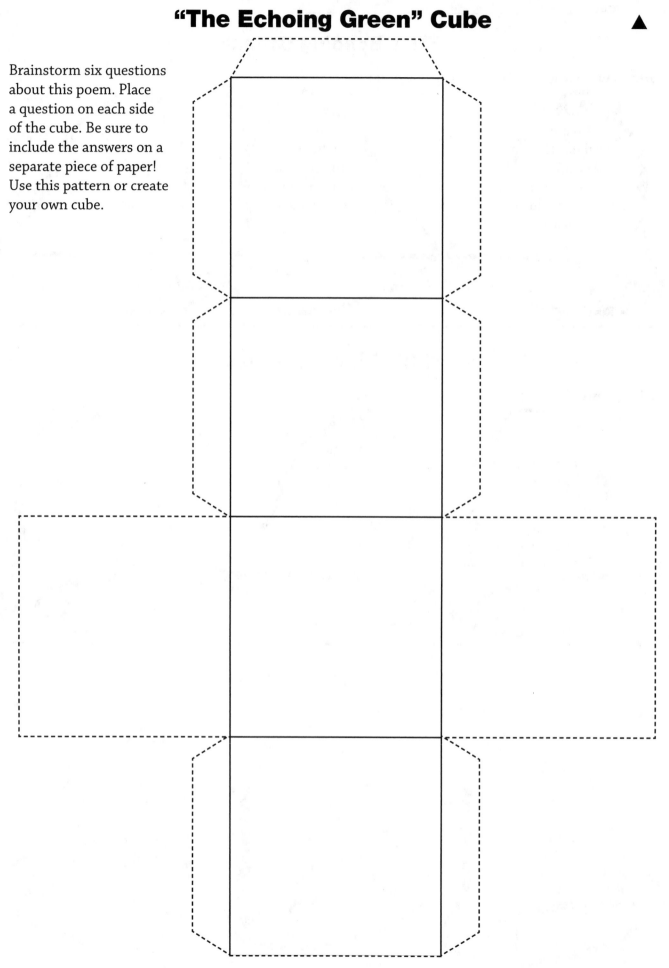

"The Echoing Green" Cube

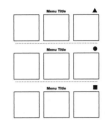

"The New Colossus"

Poetry Shape Menu

Reading Objectives Covered Through This Menu and These Activities

- Students will interpret figurative language and multiple meaning words.
- Students will make predictions based on what is read.
- Students will use resources and references to build meaning.

Writing Objectives Covered Through This Menu and These Activities

- Students will write to express their feelings, reflect, inform, explain, describe, or narrate.
- Students will use vivid language.

Materials Needed by Students for Completion

- "The New Colossus" by Emma Lazarus, see page 173
- Large lined index cards (for instruction cards) ▲
- DVD or VHS recorder (for commercials ●, video ■)
- Microsoft PowerPoint or other slideshow software ●
- Poster board or large white paper ●

Special Notes on the Modifications of This Menu

- This menu is unique from the others, as teachers can select the number of choices based on the amount of time they plan to spend processing a particular poem. This menu is divided into three sections; the top ▲ or triangle section has activities with the most modifications, the middle ● or circle section has activities with minor modifications, and the lower ■ or square section has activities that offer the most extension. If the goal is to have students create one product for the poem, then the teacher can provide each student with a strip of an appropriate level of options. For a more in-depth study, the teacher can provide the entire menu and students select one option from each section of the menu.

Special Notes on the Use of This Menu

- This menu gives students the opportunity to create commercials and videos. Although students enjoy producing their own videos, there often are difficulties obtaining the equipment and scheduling the use of a video recorder. This activity can be modified by allowing students to act out the product (like a play) or, if students have the technology, allowing them to produce a webcam version of their product.

Time Frame

- 1 week—Students are given the menu before the poem is read. The teacher will go over all of the options for the menu and have students indicate each option that represents the activity they are most interested in completing. The teacher may assign the menu as independent work or choose to allow students time to work after other work is finished.
- 1–2 days—The teacher chooses a strip for each student to complete based on his or her specific needs. The student selects one of the activities on the strip and works on it for independent practice.

Suggested Forms

- All-purpose rubric
- Student presentation rubric

The New Colossus

by Emma Lazarus

Not like the brazen giant of Greek fame,
With conquering limbs astride from land to land;
Here at our sea-washed, sunset gates shall stand
A mighty woman with a torch, whose flame
Is the imprisoned lightning, and her name
Mother of Exiles. From her beacon-hand
Glows world-wide welcome; her mild eyes command
The air-bridged harbor that twin cities frame.
"Keep, ancient lands, your storied pomp!" cries she
With silent lips. "Give me your tired, your poor,
Your huddled masses yearning to be free,
The wretched refuse of your teeming shore.
Send these, the homeless, tempest-tost to me,
I lift my lamp beside the golden door!"

"The New Colossus"

Directions: Select one of the following options.   ▲

Create a picture dictionary for at least eight interesting words in the poem.

Make an instruction card that explains how to write a sonnet.

Write a paragraph to summarize what this poem is telling readers.

"The New Colossus"

Directions: Select one of the following options.   ●

Record a commercial that uses lines from this poem to convince people to visit the Statue of Liberty.

Research the Statue of Liberty. Prepare a PowerPoint presentation about her; include lines from the poem in your presentation.

Design a poster that explains why the Statue of Liberty is called the "Mother of Exiles."

"The New Colossus"

Directions: Select one of the following options.   ■

This is a special kind of poem called a sonnet. Select an important monument or national treasure and write a sonnet about it.

Select the most important line from this poem. Record a video to talk about this line and why you picked it.

Pretend you are the Statue of Liberty. Write a diary entry to discuss how you feel about this poem and what it says about you.

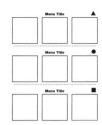

"Fog"

Poetry Shape Menu

Reading Objectives Covered Through This Menu and These Activities

- Students will interpret figurative language and multiple meaning words.
- Students will make predictions based on what is read.
- Students will use resources and references to build meaning.

Writing Objectives Covered Through This Menu and These Activities

- Students will write to express their feelings, reflect, inform, explain, describe, or narrate.
- Students will use vivid language.

Materials Needed by Students for Completion

- "Fog" by Carl Sandburg (see http://www.poemhunter.com/poem/fog)
- DVD or VHS recorder (for videos) ▲
- Magazines (for collages) ●
- Poster board or large white paper ● ■

Special Notes on the Modifications of This Menu

- This menu is unique from the others, as teachers can select the number of choices based on the amount of time they plan to spend processing a particular poem. This menu is divided into three sections; the top ▲ or triangle section has activities with the most modifications, the middle ● or circle section has activities with minor modifications, and the lower ■ or square section has activities that offer the most extension. If the goal is to have students create one product for the poem, then the teacher can provide each student with a strip of an appropriate level of options. For a more in-depth study, the teacher can provide the entire menu and students select one option from each section of the menu.

Special Notes on the Use of This Menu

- This menu gives students the opportunity to create a video of them reading a poem. Although students enjoy producing their own videos, there often are difficulties obtaining the equipment and scheduling the use of a video recorder. This activity can be modified by allowing students to read the poem "live" or, if students have the technology, allowing them to produce a webcam version of their poem.

Time Frame

- 1 week—Students are given the menu before the poem is read. The teacher will go over all of the options for the menu and have students indicate each option that represents the activity they are most interested in completing. The teacher may assign the menu as independent work or choose to allow students time to work after other work is finished.

- 1–2 days—The teacher chooses a strip for each student to complete based on his or her specific needs. The student selects one of the activities on the strip and works on it for independent practice.

Suggested Forms

- All-purpose rubric

Name: _____

"Fog"

Directions: Select one of the following options.   ▲

Choose an image for this poem. Tell why you selected that picture.

Record a video in which you read the poem "Fog" with feeling.

Retell this poem as a story, be sure and use different words.

- -

"Fog"

Directions: Select one of the following options.   ●

Turn this poem into a song and sing it for your classmates. You may repeat lines in your song.

Create a collage of words and pictures that represent the tone of this poem.

Make a drawing to illustrate the meaning of this poem.

- -

"Fog"

Directions: Select one of the following options.   ■

Design a poster that shares at least eight other examples (from poetry or stories) in which animals are used to describe nonliving things.

Write your own poem that uses a zoo animal to describe a nonliving thing.

Write a story about someone who is in the city on the day this poem took place.